Mastering Android Game Development with Unity

Exploit the advanced concepts of Unity to develop intriguing, high-end Android games

Siddharth Shekar
Wajahat Karim

BIRMINGHAM - MUMBAI

Mastering Android Game Development with Unity

First published: May 2017

Production reference: 1180517

Published by Packt Publishing Ltd.
Livery Place
35 Livery Street
Birmingham
B3 2PB, UK.

ISBN 978-1-78355-077-7

www.packtpub.com

Credits

Authors
Siddharth Shekar
Wajahat Karim

Reviewers
Asema Hassan
Engin Polat

Acquisition Editor
Shweta Pant

Content Development Editor
Zeeyan Pinheiro

Technical Editor
Pavan Ramchandani

Copy Editor
Safis Editing

Project Coordinator
Vaidehi Sawant

Proofreader
Safis Editing

Indexer
Pratik Shirodkar

Graphics
Abhinash Sahu

Production Coordinator
Aparna Bhagat

About the Authors

Siddharth Shekar is a game developer with over 5 years of experience in the game development industry and 11 years of experience in C++, C#, and other programming languages. He is adept at graphics libraries and game engines such as Unity and Unreal Engine. He has also published games on the app stores of iOS, Android, Amazon, and Windows.

Siddharth is the author of the books *Learning Cocos2d-x Game Development, Learning iOS 8 Game Development Using Swift,* and *Cocos2d Cross-Platform Game Development Cookbook* and the technical reviewer for *iOS Programming Cookbook,* all by Packt Publishing.

Currently, he is a lecturer at the games department at Media Design School, Auckland, New Zealand. He teaches graphics programming and PlayStation 4/PS Vita native game development and mentors final year production students.

To know more about Media Design School on their website. You can also find Siddharth on Twitter at @sidshekar.

> *I would like to thank my parents for supporting me in everything that I choose to do. I would also like to thank Media Design School for encouraging me to continue working on this book. Finally, I would like to thank Packt for putting this book together and offering me the opportunity to write this book.*

Wajahat Karim is a seasoned mobile app and game developer with extensive experience in diversified technologies, as well as more than 7 years of software development experience.

Wajahat received his information and communication systems engineering degree from the NUST School of Electrical Engineering and Computer Sciences (SEECS), Islamabad, Pakistan. He has been working on games since he was 14 years old and is skilled in many platforms, including Android SDK, AndEngine, Adobe Flash, Adobe AIR, Game Maker, and Unity3D.

He is skilled, not only in programming and coding, but also in computer graphic designing tools such as Adobe Photoshop, Adobe Illustrator, Adobe Flash, and Autodesk Maya. Recently, he also worked with the government of Oman in Muscat, to create a real-time election monitoring app for Android and iOS for their Shura Elections, 2015. He has run multiple startups from time to time and has also worked in a virtual reality and augmented reality startup.

Currently, besides being a full-time development manager at a multinational company, he is working with a startup that allows Android developers to boost their app growth and reward their users through in-app perks.

Wajahat has deep passion in game development, entrepreneurship, and writing. He has previously coauthored the book *Learning Android Intents* by Packt Publishing.

You can reach Wajahat on his personal website.

First of all, I would like to thank to ALLAH (the Almighty) for everything and this life. I would like to thank a very good friend of mine, Fazal Hayat aka Faizi, who helped me initiate this book and made me believe that I could complete this book. I would also like to thank my lovely sisters, Navera Karim and Sumera Aijaz, who have always been proud of me and have always encouraged and motivated me to pursue my dreams and focus on the book. Not to forget, I would like to thank my father, Abdul Karim Memon, and my aunt who is more than a mother to me for their unlimited prayers, unconditional love, and untiring efforts to make me what I am today. I would also like to thank my friends, Ayaz Ahmed, Sheeraz Ahmed, Fayaz Ahmed, Azizullah Memon, Mubashir Hassan, Ali Hussain, Arslan Abro, and the new one on this list, Hasan Ali, who are more than brothers to me and add color to my life, making it funny and enjoyable.

A deep, heartfelt thanks goes to my wife, Gul Sanober, for her tireless and unconditional support and cooperation, which helped me focus on this book, and for her ongoing support that allows me to do what I truly enjoy in life. I have taken away a lot of her deserved hours to author this book, and I am grateful and proud to have her in my life as my partner.

Last but not least, I would like to say a big thank you to Packt Publishing for their support, their understanding throughout the book, and with their complete cooperation, their help in setting this whole project in motion, and believing in me for this book.

About the Reviewers

Asema Hassan is a game developer, AI researcher, and tutor. She is currently writing her master's thesis at Otto von Guericke University, Magdeburg, Germany. Her major research focus is on artificial intelligence in games. She also works part time at the German Center for Neurodegenerative Diseases, where she develops 3D VR simulations in Unity along with her team.

She previously worked in Pakistan's game industry for almost 3 years. At *Agnitus*, she worked as a software engineer for more than 2 years and developed various 2D/2.5D games for Android/iOS. She has deep knowledge of Unity Engine, C#, and C++. She is also a supervisor for the PakGamers community, where her main responsibility is to guide new students on the game development process.

She likes to travel a lot and take photographs. You can find out more about her on `http://a semahassan.blogspot.de`.

I would like to thank Packt Publishing for giving me a chance to be a reviewer on this book and would also like to appreciate all efforts of the authors to make this book a good read.

Engin Polat has been involved in many large-scale and medium-scale projects on .NET technologies as a developer, architect, and consultant and has won many awards since 1999.

Since 2008, he has been conducting training for many large enterprises in Turkey on Windows development, web development, distributed application development, software architecture, mobile development, cloud development, and so on.

Apart from this, he organizes seminars and events in many universities in Turkey on .NET technologies, Windows platform development, cloud development, web development, game development, and so on.

He shares his experiences on his personal blog (http://www.enginpolat.com).

He has MCP, MCAD, MCSD, MCDBA, and MCT certifications.

In 2012, he was recognized as a Windows development MVP (Most Valuable Professional) by Microsoft, and in 2017, he got recognized as a Visual Studio and Development Technologies MVP too.

Between 2013 and 2015, he was recognized as a Nokia Developer Champion; very few people in the world are given this award. In 2015, he was recognized as the regional director by Microsoft.

He has worked on several books by Packt, including *Mastering Cross Platform with Xamarin, Xamarin Blueprints, Xamarin by Example,* and *Mastering Xamarin UI Development*.

I'd like to thank my dear wife, Yeliz, and my beautiful daughter, Melis Ada, for all the support they gave me while I was working on this book. I also want to give a warm welcome to the newest member of my family, my dear son, Utku Ege.

www.PacktPub.com

For support files and downloads related to your book, please visit www.PacktPub.com.

Did you know that Packt offers eBook versions of every book published, with PDF and ePub files available? You can upgrade to the eBook version at www.PacktPub.comand as a print book customer, you are entitled to a discount on the eBook copy. Get in touch with us at service@packtpub.com for more details.

At www.PacktPub.com, you can also read a collection of free technical articles, sign up for a range of free newsletters and receive exclusive discounts and offers on Packt books and eBooks.

https://www.packtpub.com/mapt

Get the most in-demand software skills with Mapt. Mapt gives you full access to all Packt books and video courses, as well as industry-leading tools to help you plan your personal development and advance your career.

Why subscribe?

- Fully searchable across every book published by Packt
- Copy and paste, print, and bookmark content
- On demand and accessible via a web browser

Customer Feedback

Thanks for purchasing this Packt book. At Packt, quality is at the heart of our editorial process. To help us improve, please leave us an honest review on this book's Amazon page at https://www.amazon.com/dp/1783550775.

If you'd like to join our team of regular reviewers, you can e-mail us at customerreviews@packtpub.com. We award our regular reviewers with free eBooks and videos in exchange for their valuable feedback. Help us be relentless in improving our products!

Table of Contents

Preface

Unity has come a long way from its humble beginnings; however, since the last couple of years, it has almost become an industry-wide used tool that almost all independent game developers use to develop their games. It is very easy to use to develop prototypes, and when you have a successful idea, it is flexible enough to expand the small prototype to a full-fledged game.

Despite its professional capacity, Unity is so simple to use that even a complete novice person can develop a basic game within a matter of hours. And with a little more effort, a very polished game can be developed with excellent lighting and animation.

With the current version, Unity makes game development even more accessible to everyone.

In this book, we will cover a variety of topics both in 2D and 3D game development. We will see how to develop a game similar to JetPack Joyride in 2D, and a 3D fighting game with full 3D animation, lighting, and camera. We will also see how to add buttons, text, and screen transitions. Finally, once we have created the game, we will see how to monetize it by adding in-app purchases and ads.

What this book covers

Chapter 1, *Introduction to Android Game Development with Unity3D*, covers the basic concepts of Android game development, a brief history of Android games, the building blocks of Android games in Unity3D, and the basic flow of games.

Chapter 2, *Finishing the Perky Penguin 2D Game*, extends 2D game development by finishing the Jetpack Joyride clone game. The chapter introduces various topics, such as particle systems, camera management, prefabs, animations, triggers, colliders, and basic GUI systems.

Chapter 3, *Player Character for Action Fighting Game*, covers the basic setup for 3D action fighting game, importing models and textures, setting rigging for the characters, applying animations on models, and controlling the player character with a virtual on-screen joystick.

Chapter 4, *Enemy Character with AI*, covers the aspect of creating the enemy model of the game from importing models to applying animations to decision making with AI.

Chapter 5, *Gameplay, UI, and Effects*, shows how to finish the gameplay loop, add a UI, add text for scoring the game, and add particle effects to the game.

Chapter 6, *GameScene and SceneFlow*, covers the creation of MainMenu Scene, explains Options Scene, and demonstrates how to transition between the scenes in the game.

Chapter 7, *Gamestats, Social, IAP and Ad integration*, demonstrates how to save in-game progress, add social media integration such as Facebook and Twitter, ad integration, and In-App purchases to add monetization.

Chapter 8, *Sound, Finishing Touches, and Publishing*, lets us add finishing touches to the game and add sound. We will see how to run the game on the device and publish the game to the Android Play Store.

What you need for this book

You will need the latest version of Unity, which you can download from their website, and a computer that can run Unity. A basic understanding of C# is required as the code in this book is written in C#. Although the game can run on an Android emulator, to see the actual performance of the game, an Android device would be required.

Who this book is for

This book is geared toward novice or intermediate Unity3D developers who want to expand their knowledge of Unity3D and create high-end, complex Android games. You are expected to have a basic or intermediate understanding of Unity3D, working with its environment, basic concepts such as Game Objects and Prefabs, Unity Scripting using C# or JavaScript, and how to develop basic 2D/3D games using Unity3D.

The book is very useful for those Unity developers who have created basic/simple games for Android and want to learn the ins and outs and core components of high-end complex games that have features such as detailed animations, multiple levels, character abilities, enemy weaknesses, intelligent AI, achievements, leaderboards, and a lot more.

Conventions

In this book, you will find a number of text styles that distinguish between different kinds of information. Here are some examples of these styles and an explanation of their meaning.

Code words in text, database table names, folder names, filenames, file extensions, pathnames, dummy URLs, user input, and Twitter handles are shown as follows: "The bIsDefending variable is the same as that we defined as a parameter in Animation Controller."

A block of code is set as follows:

```
private Animator anim;
// Use this for initialization

void Start () {
    anim = GetComponent<Animator>();
} // start
```

When we wish to draw your attention to a particular part of a code block, the relevant lines or items are set in bold:

```
if (pAnim.GetBool("tIsPunching")){
    if (anim.GetBool("bEnemyIsDefending") == false) {
        Debug.Log("enemy got hit");
        anim.SetTrigger("tEnemyGotHit");
        anim.SetBool("bEnemyIsDefending", true);
        health -= pScript.damage;
    }
}
```

Any command-line input or output is written as follows:

```
C:\Program Files\Unity\Editor\Unity.exe
```

New terms and **important words** are shown in bold. Words that you see on the screen, for example, in menus or dialog boxes, appear in the text like this: "Unity lets developers manage these components of each game object through the **Inspector** panel."

Warnings or important notes appear in a box like this.

 Tips and tricks appear like this.

Reader feedback

Feedback from our readers is always welcome. Let us know what you think about this book—what you liked or disliked. Reader feedback is important for us as it helps us develop titles that you will really get the most out of.

To send us general feedback, simply e-mail feedback@packtpub.com, and mention the book's title in the subject of your message.

If there is a topic that you have expertise in and you are interested in either writing or contributing to a book, see our author guide at www.packtpub.com/authors.

Customer support

Now that you are the proud owner of a Packt book, we have a number of things to help you to get the most from your purchase.

Downloading the example code

You can download the example code files for this book from your account at http://www.packtpub.com. If you purchased this book elsewhere, you can visit http://www.packtpub.com/support and register to have the files e-mailed directly to you.

You can download the code files by following these steps:

1. Log in or register to our website using your e-mail address and password.
2. Hover the mouse pointer on the **SUPPORT** tab at the top.
3. Click on **Code Downloads & Errata**.
4. Enter the name of the book in the **Search** box.

5. Select the book for which you're looking to download the code files.

6. Choose from the drop-down menu where you purchased this book from.

7. Click on **Code Download**.

Once the file is downloaded, please make sure that you unzip or extract the folder using the latest version of:

- WinRAR / 7-Zip for Windows
- Zipeg / iZip / UnRarX for Mac
- 7-Zip / PeaZip for Linux

The code bundle for the book is also hosted on GitHub at `https://github.com/PacktPublishing/Mastering-Android-Game-Development-with-Unity`. We also have other code bundles from our rich catalog of books and videos available at `https://github.com/PacktPublishing/`. Check them out!

Downloading the color images of this book

We also provide you with a PDF file that has color images of the screenshots/diagrams used in this book. The color images will help you better understand the changes in the output. You can download this file from `http://www.packtpub.com/sites/default/files/downloads/MasteringAndroidGameDevelopmentwithUnity_ColorImages.pdf`.

Errata

Although we have taken every care to ensure the accuracy of our content, mistakes do happen. If you find a mistake in one of our books—maybe a mistake in the text or the code—we would be grateful if you could report this to us. By doing so, you can save other readers from frustration and help us improve subsequent versions of this book. If you find any errata, please report them by visiting `http://www.packtpub.com/submit-errata`, selecting your book, clicking on the **Errata Submission Form** link, and entering the details of your errata. Once your errata are verified, your submission will be accepted and the errata will be uploaded to our website or added to any list of existing errata under the Errata section of that title.

To view the previously submitted errata, go to `https://www.packtpub.com/books/content/support` and enter the name of the book in the search field. The required information will appear under the **Errata** section.

Piracy

Piracy of copyrighted material on the Internet is an ongoing problem across all media. At Packt, we take the protection of our copyright and licenses very seriously. If you come across any illegal copies of our works in any form on the Internet, please provide us with the location address or website name immediately so that we can pursue a remedy.

Please contact us at copyright@packtpub.com with a link to the suspected pirated material.

We appreciate your help in protecting our authors and our ability to bring you valuable content.

Questions

If you have a problem with any aspect of this book, you can contact us at questions@packtpub.com, and we will do our best to address the problem.

1

Introduction to Android Game Development with Unity3D

In today's era of smartphones, which once was the era of computers, almost everyone on the planet is holding a smartphone in their hands. About 1 billion Android phones have been sold in 2014, which is a huge audience for developers who work on Android. These developers put their effort into creating high utility apps, which solves the problems of their users or addicting and fun games and allows players to pass the time having fun and enjoying good interactive experiences. This book is mainly focused on covering the latter part, creating addictive fun games, by using a very famous game engine called Unity3D.

This chapter includes the following topics.

- Introduction to Android
- Unity3D and Game Engines
- Basics of Unity Game Development
- Configuration of Empty Game Projects
- Starting the Perky Penguin Game
- Adding the Penguin to the Game

Introduction to Android

Android is a Linux-based operating system, which makes it open source software distributed under the Apache License Agreement by Google Inc. Due to its open source nature, other phone vendors have started porting the Android operating system on their newly created phones, which contributed to a very varied smartphone market for consumers. Starting from the first version of Android, this operating system has gained a good level of maturity, making it more reliable, secure, and stable operating system for smartphones. Let's have a look on some popular versions of Android in the next section.

Android versions

Year by year, Android has increased its maturity level with each new version. Every version introduced new set of features from the user interface to customizations to flexibility to security. In terms of names, these versions are based on names of candy, chocolates, and other sweet stuff, such as Kitkat, Lollipop, and Marshmallow, but that's what makes Android a little more understandable to consumers and developers as well.

It is an interesting fact that the versions of Android are in alphabetical order. Starting off from *Apple Pie 1.0* and then *Banana Bread 1.1*, it made its way towards *Nougat* with a completely coherent of alphabetical sequence maintaining the legacy.

The following table highlights the main features of the different Android versions with their API levels as well:

Android version	Version name	Main features	API level	Release month
1.0 G1	Banana Bread	GPS, Bluetooth, Multitasking, Google Services, Android Play Store	2	February 2008
1.5	Cupcake	Search Box, Revamped Android Play Store, Camera, Gestures	3	April 2009
1.6	Donut	Onscreen Keyboard, Home Screen Widgets, Folders	4	September 2009
2.0.x	Éclair	Multiple User Accounts, Flash Support, Zoom Feature, Bluetooth 2.1	5, 6, and 7	October 2009

2.2.x	Froyo	USB tethering, Hotspot support, Adobe Flash, Voice Dialling	8	May 2010
2.3.x	Gingerbread	New Copy/Paste, WebM, NFC, Front Camera	9, 10	December 2010
3.x	Honeycomb	3D Graphics, Redesigned UI, Video Chatting, Bluetooth tethering, 3G, 4G	11, 12, and 13	February 2011
4.0.x	Ice Cream Sandwich	Virtual buttons, Face Unlock, Native Camera Features, Face Detection, Android Beam, Wi-Fi Direct	14 and 15	October 2011
4.1 - 4.3	Jelly Bean	Expandable Notifications, Google Now	16, 17, and 18	July 2012
4.4	Kit Kat	Major Design Interface Update, Translucent Status bar, Immersive Mode, Wireless Printing	19 and 20	October 2013
5.0	Lollipop	Redesigned UI with Material, Lock Screen Notifications, Guest mode, Battery Saver mode	21	October 2014
6.0	Marshmellow	Fingerprint security support, Doze mode for battery saving, App standby mode, Enhanced App permission	23	October 5, 2015
7.0	Nougat	Multi window view, VR support	24, and 25	August 22, 2016

Table 1.1: Era of operating systems from Android Cupcake to Lollipop

The table only shows the changes made by Android operating system's developer, Google Inc. But due to Android's open source nature, other mobile manufacturing companies have also changed and introduced new features and modifications into Android. For example, Samsung has made a custom touch interface called TouchWiz, and HTC has made a custom user interface called HTC Sense. Similarly, Sony has introduced a custom user interface called **TimeScape**.

Figure 1.1 Latest Android phones launched in year 2014

Google Play - the market store for Android

After the introduction of smart phones, the concept of market store came to existence in software technology, which revolutionized the mobile development industry. A significant role was played by Google Play in that revolution of mobile apps and games. Google Play is the largest market store in smartphones, with more than 2.2 million Android apps, games, books, music, shows, and more. These apps and games have been downloaded more than 50 billion times up to this point, and that marks a huge milestone achieved by Google in just 8 years of Android. You can check out Google Play at `http://play.google.com`.

Google Music, Google Movies & TV, Google Books, and Google
Magazines are available in only limited countries.

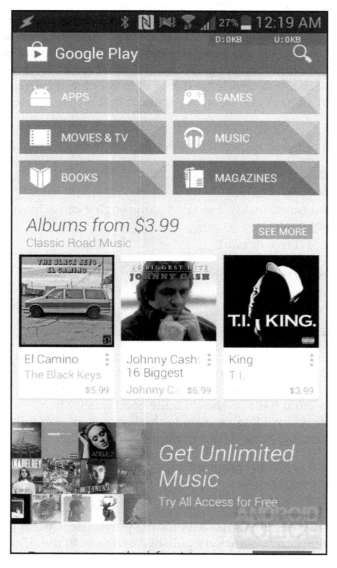

Figure 1.2 Google Play on an Android device

Unity3D and game engines

A **game engine** is a software framework designed for the creation and development of video games. Many tools and frameworks are available for game designers and developers to code a game quickly and easily without building from the ground up. As time passed by, game engines have become more mature and easy for developers, with feature-rich environments. Starting from native code frameworks for Android such as Unity, Unreal, Cocos2D-x, LibGDX , and so on, the game engines started providing clean user interfaces and drag-drop functionalities to make game development easier for developers. These engines include lots of the tools which are different in user interface, features, porting, and many more things but all have one thing in common; that is they create video games at the end.

We will discuss some of the most popular game engines in this section by comparing those on the basis of:

- User Interface and environment like how easy it is to learn and develop games.
- Features and functionality like what game engine can achieve and do and on what level of quality.
- Pricing like is it free or paid.

Let's get into more details with this comparison.

Unreal Engine

Unreal Engine (`http://www.unrealengine.com`) is a game engine developed by Epic Games. It was an in-house game engine of Epic Games and was first showcased in 1998 first person shooter game Unreal. Unreal Engine is mostly used for creating first-person or third-person shooter games but it has also shown quite good quality in other genres such as stealth, MMORPGs etc. Unreal Engine includes high degree of portability and easy interface features with more logic and behaviors written in C++ language.

The latest release called as Unreal Engine 4 supports almost all platforms supported by Unity including Windows, Xbox One, Windows RT, OS X, Linux, PlayStation 4, iOS, Android, Ouya, and browsers using WebGL.

Unreal Engine 4 was released in March 2014 for the public use. Unreal Engine has nice user interface and navigation controls are very polished and easy to use. Unreal Engine provides very easy flow and interface to create first person shooter games and contains features to produce AAA quality game including real-time global illumination using voxel cone tracing, eliminating pre-computed lighting.

You can download the engine and use it for everything from game development, education, architecture, and visualization to VR, film and animation. When you ship a game or application, you pay a 5% royalty on gross revenue after the first $3,000 per product, per quarter Unreal Engine's learning curve is a little high so it's not best suited for new aspiring game developers:

Figure 1.3 Unreal Engine 4 Interface

Adobe Flash professional

Adobe Flash (formerly called as Macromedia Flash) (http://www.adobe.com) is a multimedia and software platform used for creating vector graphics, animations, games, and rich internet applications (RIAs) that can be viewed, played, and executed in Adobe Flash Player. The Flash is widely used for creating animations and mostly advertisements for web browsers but its use of creating games is declined very heavily in recent years by HTML5 framework.

There was a time when Adobe Flash was most popular game engine for online browser games and made a quite big wave of independent game developers creating games for online portals such as Kongregate and Miniclip.

The Adobe Flash includes very easy interface to create amazing and robust animations allowing artists to create vector art directly in the editor. It also supports Adobe Illustrator and Adobe Photoshop layers as well to make it easy integrated with vector art and animations. Adobe Flash allowed developers to port their games and animations from browsers to Desktops (Mac and Windows), Android, and iOS using Adobe AIR framework but couldn't grasp the much attention of game developers and artists due to low performance on end devices.

Adobe Flash has a Free 30-day trial but once the trial is finished you must buy a license unlike other engines discussed in this section.

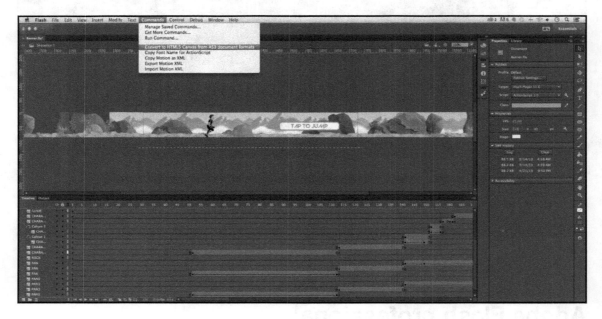

Figure 1.4 Adobe Flash CC Interface

Game Maker Studio

Game Maker Studio (originally names Animo and later Game Maker) is an event-driven game creation system created by Mark Overmars in Delphi programming language in 1999. Originally created for 2D animations, it quickly moved up high on to being a very robust and easy-to-use drag-drop tool for creating 2D games.

Game Maker Studio uses pre-defined events to create actions in the game, which makes it very easy for developers to create games without needing prior knowledge of programming and coding stuff. The tool comes with a sandboxed language called **Game Maker Language (GML)**, which allows developers to define custom and more complex behaviors for their games.

The Game Maker Studio comes with a clean and slick user interface that lets developers build and deploy their games on Windows, macOS X, Ubuntu, HTML5, Android, iOS, Windows Phone 8, and Tizen. The latest version also introduced Xbox One and PlayStation deployment.

Tizen is the open source operating system (OS) of everything, including mobiles, wearables, in-vehicle infotainment, and TV.

Figure 1.5 Game Maker Studio Interface

Unity3D

Unity (`http://unity3d.com`) is cross-platform game engine developed by Unity Technologies. It made its first public announcement at Apple's Worldwide Developers Conference in 2005 and supported only game development for Mac OS, but since then it has been extended to target more than 15 platforms for desktop, mobile, and consoles. It is notable for its one-click ability to port games on multiple platforms, including BlackBerry 10, Windows Phone 10, Windows 10, OS X, Linux, Android, iOS, Unity Web Player (including Facebook), Adobe Flash, PlayStation 3, PlayStation 4, PlayStation Vita, Xbox 360, Xbox One, Wii U, and Wii.

Unity has a fantastic interface that lets the developers manage the project really efficiently from the get-go. It has nice drag-drop functionality with connecting behavior scripts written in C# and Boo (a dialect of JavaScript) to define the custom logic and functionality with visual objects quite easily. Unity has been proven quite easy to learn for the new developers who are just starting out with game development and now more large studios have also started it using, and that is also for good reasons.

Unity is one of those engines that provides support for both 2D and 3D games without putting developers in trouble and confusion. It has vast collection of online tutorials, great documentation, and a very helpful community of developers. Also, Unity has the Asset Store, where developers sell reusable components of Unity to reduce the development time and efforts for other developers. You can check Unity Asset Store at `http://assetstore.un ity3d.com`.

Unity Plus and Pro are available for a fee, and Unity Personal has no fee; it is available any use to individuals or companies with less than US $100,000 of annual gross revenue. For more information, visit the Unity store at `https://store.unity.com/`:

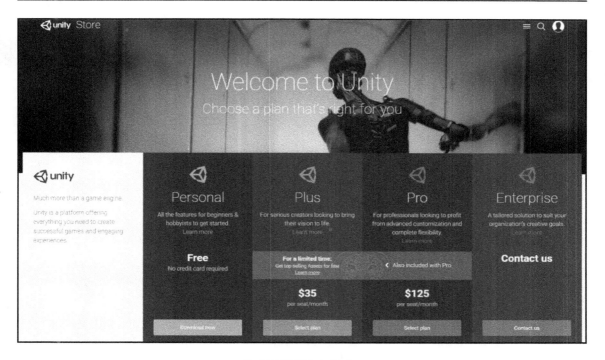

Figure 1.6 Unity3D Engine Interface

Features of Unity3D

Unity is a game development ecosystem of powerful rendering engine, intuitive tools, rapid workflows for 2D and 3D games, all-in-one deployment support, and thousands of already created free and paid assets with a helpful developers community. The feature list includes the following:

- Easy workflow, allowing developers to rapidly assemble scenes in an intuitive editor workspace
- Quality game creation, such as AAA visuals, high-definition audio, and full-throttle action, without any glitches on screen
- Dedicated tools for both 2D and 3D game creation with shared conventions to make it easy for developers
- A very unique and flexible animation system to create natural animations in very less time

- Smooth frame rate with reliable performance on all the platforms developers publish their games
- One-click ability to deploy to all platforms from desktops to browsers to mobiles to consoles, within minutes
- Reduce the time of development by using already created reusable assets available on the huge Asset Store

In summary, compared to other game engines Unity is developer-friendly, easy to use, free for independent developers, and feature-rich game engine. In next section, we will see some amazing features of Unity3D.

Basics of Unity game development

Before delving into the details of Unity3D and game development concepts, let's have a look at some of the basics of Unity 5.6 We will go through the unity interface, menu items, using assets, creating scenes, and publishing builds.

 This section is required for all new developers who have very little or no knowledge of Unity and want to learn basics of game development using Unity. If you are already familiar with Unity basics, you can skip this section.

Unity editor interface

When you first time launch Unity 5.6, you will be presented with an editor containing a few panels on left, right, and bottom of the screen. There's nothing to worry from these panels. The following image shows the editor interface when it's first launched:

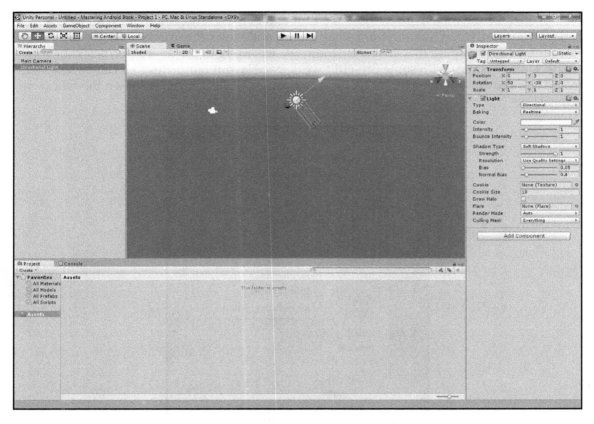

Figure 1.7 Unity 5 Editor Interface at first launch

First of all, take the time to look over the editor and become a little familiar with it. The Unity editor is divided into different small panels and views that can be dragged around, resulting in a workspace that can be customized, according to the developer/designer's needs. Unity 5 comes with some pre-built workspace layout templates that can be selected from **Layout** drop-down menu in the top-right corner of the screen, as shown the following screenshot:

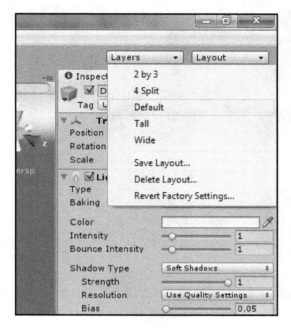

Figure 1.8 Unity 5 editor layouts

The layout currently displayed in the editor is the **Default** layout. You can select these layouts and see how the editor's interface changes and how different panels are placed in different positions in each layout. This book uses the **2 by 3** workspace layout for the game.

The following screenshot shows the 2 by 3 workspace with the names of the views and panels highlighted:

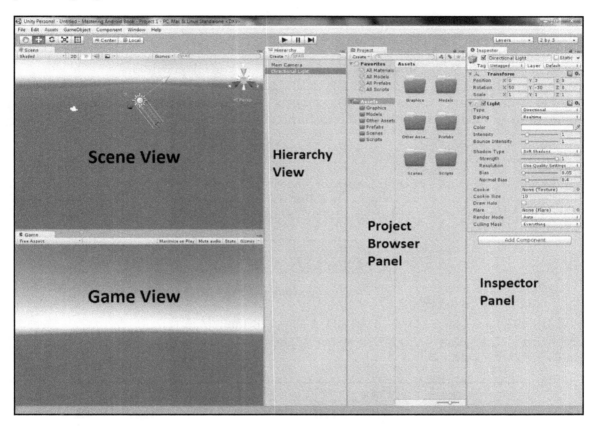

Figure 1.9 Unity 5 2 by 3 layout with views and panel names

As you can see in the preceding screenshot, Unity editor contains different views and panels. Every panel and view has a specific purpose, which is described in the following section.

Scene View

Scene View is the whole stage for the game development, and it contains every asset in the game from a tiny point to any heavy 3D model. Scene View is used to select and position environments, characters, enemies, the player, camera, and all other objects that can be placed on the stage for the game. All those objects, which can be placed and shown in the game, are called as **GameObjects**. The scene view allows developers to manipulate game objects such as selecting, scaling, rotating, deleting, and moving. In simple words, Scene View is the interactive sandbox for the developers and designers. The Scene View provides some controls, such as navigation and transformation.

Transform tools

While developing games in Unity, you will place lots of game objects in the scene and their position, scale, and rotations, collectively called as transforms, are managed by transform tools. The following screenshot shows the transform tools:

Figure 1.10 Transform Tools

You can select any selected transform action from this toolbar and change the game object accordingly. The following figure shows the gizmo on the selected game object when a transform tool is selected:

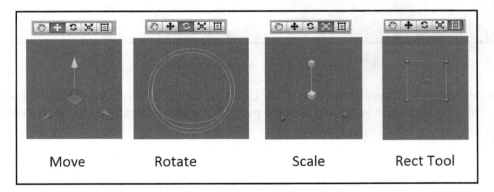

Move   Rotate   Scale   Rect Tool

Figure 1.11 Gizmos on game objects of transform Tools

These tools do exactly the same job as their names suggest; move for translation, rotate for rotation, and scale for scaling. The Rect tool on other side was introduced in Unity 4.3 when Unity got native 2D support and tools. This tool is only for 2D sprite objects for their position, scale, and rotations. You can also select these tools with keyboard shortcuts.

Scene View navigation

In the last section, we discussed how GameObjects can be transformed and navigated in the scene. But Unity being a 3D environment, it has an easy interface to view the scene from different angles, sides, and perspectives using mouse and keyboard shortcuts. You can observe the Scene Gizmo in the top-right corner of the Scene view. This gizmo is used to rotate the view according to the developer's needs. The following screenshot shows the gizmo of the scene:

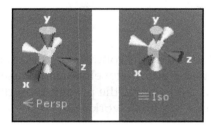

Figure 1.12 Scene Gizmo for Scene View Navigation

Every view of the scene is shown in either perspective or isometric. There is also another view for the scene which we will discuss in the next section.

Scene View control bar

The control bar is shown at the top of the Scene View and it gives the developer more control to navigate through their scenes and create games easily. This bar includes options such as enabling/disabling gizmos, sounds, and selecting view modes. The important part of this bar is the 2D mode button, as shown in the following screenshot:

Figure 1.13 control bar of Scene View

The 2D mode button is a toggle button; when turned on; it disables the z-axis of the view and show the game from 2D perspective. It is highly used option while creating 2D games in Unity. On the right side of the bar, there is a text box for search. This lets developers search the game objects from the current scene and allows them to quickly work.

Game View

The Game View is the final representation of how your game will look when published and deployed on the target devices, and it is rendered from the cameras of the scene. This view is connected to the Play Mode navigation bar at the top of the whole Unity workspace, as shown in the following screenshot:

Figure 1.14 Play mode bar

When the game is played in the editor, this control bar gets changed into blue. A very interesting feature of Unity is that it allows developers to pause the game and code while running and developers can see and change the properties, transforms etc at runtime without recompiling whole game for quick workflow.

Game View control bar

Like scene view, game view also includes a control bar on top side of the view as shown in the following figure:

Figure 1.15 Game View Control Bar

The options perform the actions as their names suggest. The Free Aspect drop-down on the left side of the bar lets developers choose any specific resolution to test their games. These resolutions and drop down options vary on the selected platform. Developers can also add their own custom resolutions and screen sizes for their targeted devices. Unity also allows developers to specify aspect ratios as well to have an idea of how the game will run on various devices with the same aspect ratio. Unity is quite powerful and easily gives cross-platform support to make their games run better on most types of devices writing code only once.

Hierarchy View

The Hierarchy View is the first point to select or handle any GameObject in the scene. This contains every game object in the current scene. This is tree-type structure allowing developers to utilize parent and child concepts on the game objects easily. The following screenshot shows a simple Hierarchy View:

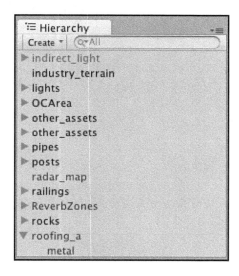

Figure 1.16 Hierarchy View

Project browser panel

This looks like a view, but it is called the **Project** browser panel. This panel is an embedded files directory in Unity and contains all the files and folders included in the game project.

Following screenshot shows a simple **Project** browser panel:

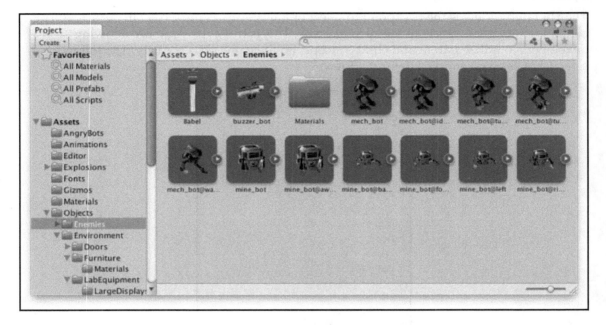

Figure 1.17 Project browser panel

The left side of the panel shows a hierarchical directory, while rest of the panel is the files or as these are called assets in Unity. Unity represents these files with different icons to differentiate these according to their file types. These files can be sprite images, textures, model files, sounds and so on. You can search any specific file by typing in the search text box. On the right side of search box, there are button controls for further filters such as animation files, audio clip files, and so on.

 An interesting thing about **Project** browser panel is that if any file is not available in the assets, then Unity starts looking for it on Unity Asset Store and presents you with available free and paid assets.

Inspector panel

This is a most important panel for development in Unity. Unity structures the game in the form of game objects and assets. These game objects further contain components such as transforms, colliders, scripts, and meshes, and so on. Unity lets developers manage these components of each game object through the inspector panel.

The following screenshot shows a simple inspector panel of a game object:

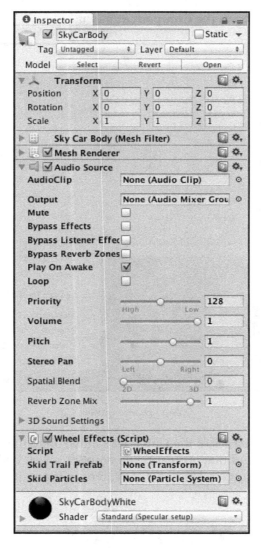

Figure 1.18 Inspector Panel

These components vary in type including physics, mesh, effects, audio, and user interface. These components can be added to any object by selecting it from the component menu. The following screenshot shows the **Component** menu:

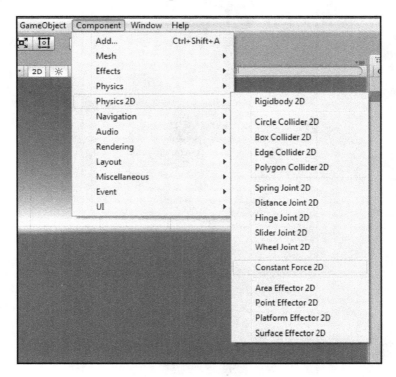

Figure 1.19 Components Menu

After covering some of the basics of the Unity, let's move on to the very first task developers do when creating a game; and that is creating an empty project. Let's discuss the configuration of empty projects in Unity for 2D games in the next section.

Configuration of empty game projects

When you start a new game, the first step is to configure an empty game project. For 2D games, creating empty games and setting up the initial environment and camera management can sometimes become a painful process. In this section, we will discuss on how to configure empty game projects for 2D games.

If you have already worked on 2D games in Unity, then you can skip this section and use the starter project of Perky Penguin from the code in the next section.

When you launch Unity 5.6, it shows a project wizard as shown in the following figure:

Figure 1.20 Project Creation Wizard

Unity has a nice and smooth user interface in its latest release, Unity 5.6. The project wizard shows a list of all the recent projects, along with their names. The most recent project is highlighted for quick opening. In the top-right side of the wizard, there are controls to create a new project from scratch and open any specific project from any directory. To guide new developers through basic concepts, the **Get started** tab offers a basic video tutorial.

Let's create new project by clicking on the **New project** button on top-right, and you will be presented with the following dialog box:

Figure 1.21 Project creation wizard

There are two text inputs, **Project name** and **Location**. Their names are self-explanatory. You will also notice **3D** and **2D** in the wizard, as shown in following figure:

Figure 1.22 Project type selection toggle

This toggle lets you tell Unity whether your project is 2D or 3D. Although this doesn't affect the project in any way while working on it, this affects default project setting for easier workflow. For example, in 3D mode, when you import any image asset into project, Unity will take it as a texture and in 2D mode, Unity will take it as a Sprite type. You can also change the mode later from the project anytime, it is not necessary to select at project creation time. By default, Unity will create project in 3D mode.

Along with 2D/3D mode, you will also notice the **Asset packages...** button at bottom on the project creation wizard. One of the best features of the Unity is the Assets support. Unity lets developers to create, distribute, and sell reusable plugins and add-ons called Unity Assets through Unity Asset Store available at `http://assetstore.unity3d.com`. Unity comes with a big collection of free assets to help you get some things done within the minutes. This button lets you choose which assets to import in the new project, shown as following:

Figure 1.23 Asset Packages Dialogue

You can select any package or multiple packages, and the new project will be created with those that have been already imported in it. For now, you don't need to import any packages. You can also import these later as you need it.

So, for the project creation wizard, we have named our project **Perky Penguin** and we have selected 2D mode. Click on the **Create project** button, and you will see the Unity interface with an empty scene and project.

The first step to follow is to make sure that you are in 2D or 3D mode. If you have selected **2D** mode, then you will see 2D toggle active on the control bar in the Scene View, as shown in the following screenshot:

Figure 1.24 Control bar in Scene View

Also, you need to check in Editor Settings to make sure that the project is in 2D mode. You can do it by going to Editor Settings by selecting **Editor** option from **Project Settings** in the **Edit** menu as shown in the following figure:

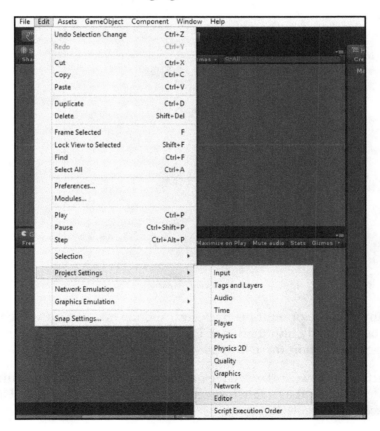

Figure 1.25 Editor Settings Menu

On selecting the **Editor** option, you will see settings in the **Inspector** panel. Make sure that **Mode** in **Default Behavior Mode** is set to **2D,** as shown in the following screenshot:

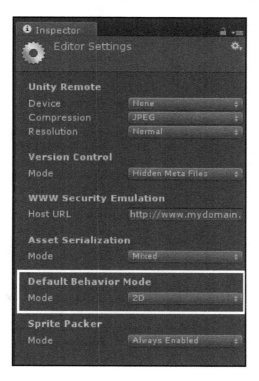

Figure 1.26 Editor Settings in Inspector Panel

You can also change it to 3D if you want Unity to interpret images as textures and enable other 3D settings by default. The last thing to make sure that the scene is in 2D mode, you need to check the camera properties. You may have already have noticed a Camera game object placed in the empty scene when creating a new project.

Select the **Camera** object and you will see its properties in inspector panel as shown in the following screenshot:

Figure 1.27 Main Camera Settings

You will notice that its **Position** will be set at (0, 0, -10) and its **Projection** setting will be as **Orthographic**.

 It is a good practice to use orthographic projection mode for 2D in unity.

Orthographic projection is a means of representing 3D objects in 2D. Orthographic views are commonly used in engineering as a means of producing object specifications that communicate dimensions unambiguously. For example, if you are looking at a larger scene with buildings then orthographic rendering gives a clear measure of distance between buildings and their relative sizes.

So, after making sure that the project is in 2D mode, let's save the scene. Unity project comes with a root directory of **Assets**, where all the assets used in project are placed. These assets can be scenes, scripts, textures, sprites, models, prefabs, or materials. There is no traditional or standard method of managing assets in Unity, and every developer has different methods. In this book, we will follow a simple method of managing assets. Our method of managing assets is to create different folders in the `Assets` directory for each type of resources. The following figure shows the directory structure in the `Assets` folder:

Figure 1.28 The Assets directory in Unity

After creating folders in Assets, let's save the empty scene with the configured camera in the **Scenes** directory with the name `PerkyPenguin_GameplayScene.unity`. Scene files have the `.unity` extension, and these files contain different game objects for camera, player, enemies, obstacles, environment, controls, and so on. Scenes are like different levels in the game. Any game can have one or more than one scenes and it is not necessary to create different scenes for each level. It is very important to note that all the scenes in the game should be added in Build settings in order to deploy them in the final package. We will discuss about deployment in more detail in the later chapters.

After saving the scene, we have only one thing left to fully configure an empty game project. That is configuring the game view so we can test our game. As this book is about Android game development, we have to set our project targeted to Android devices. Initially, the default target platform will be set to PC, iMac, and Linux standalone. You can see it in the **Build Settings** from the **File** menu as shown in the following screenshot:

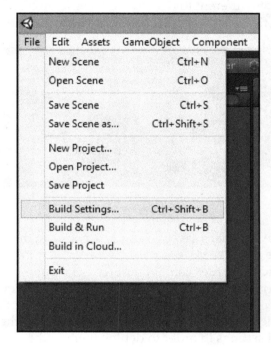

Figure 1.29 Assets Directory in Unity

You will be presented with a dialog containing all the possible platforms to build game to and all the scenes included in the game, as shown in the following screenshot:

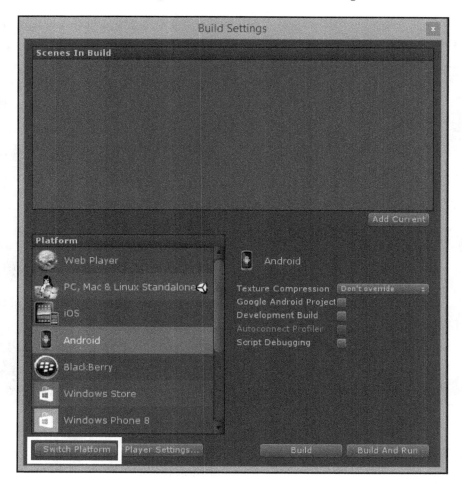

Figure 1.30 Build Settings

Select **Android** from the **Platform** list, and click on **Switch Platform** button and the project will be changed for Android devices. You might not notice anything after changing the target platform to Android but an easy way to check it is to see the resolutions list in the game view. You can do it by clicking on Free Aspect from the control bar in Game View as shown in the following figure:

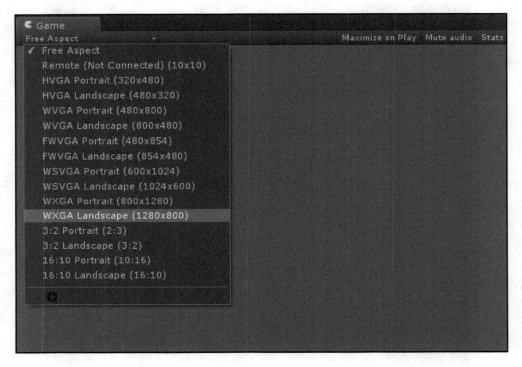

Figure 1.31 Resolution List of Android Platform

In order to create a game, that runs on all Android devices, we have to select a primary target size for viewport implementation. We have chosen 1280x800 as our target device in landscape mode. We will discuss the cross-resolution approach in details in the later chapters.

You can also add your own custom resolutions by selecting the small plus button in resolution list. It will show you a dialog to put the size of resolution either in pixels or as an aspect ratio with its name. The window is shown in the following figure:

Figure 1.32 Add Custom Resolution in Game View

Finally, after setting the project in 2D mode and changing the platform to Android with our required resolution, we have only one little job remaining that is to configure camera according to our target resolution. Select the **Main Camera** from **Hierarchy** panel, and change the **Size** in **Camera** component to 3.2 as shown in the following figure:

Figure 1.33 Camera Size

So far, a 2D Unity game project has been created with an initial directory structure and an empty scene which include a 2D configured camera in it. In the next section, we will discuss on what game will be created in this chapter and how to create any game from scratch.

Perky Penguin game

This section is all about the game which we will create throughout this chapter and Chapter 2, *Finishing the Perky Penguin 2D Game*. Our game name is **Perky Penguin** and it is a Jetpack Joyride-based game. Final game of this chapter is shown as following:

Figure 1.34 Perky Penguin Gameplay

Perky Penguin is inspired from Jetpack Joyride game. Jetpack Joyride is a 2011 side-scrolling endless runner and action video game created by Halfbrick Studios. It was originally released in 2011 for iOS devices on App Store but it has been ported to many systems including Facebook, Android, Flash, PlayStation, Blackberry, and Windows Phone.

 Jetpack Joyride game was titled **Machine Gun Jetpack** during development.

The reason to create a Jetpack Joyride type game for this book is to teach the developers the perspective and methods of how 2D games are created in Unity from scratch. As Jetpack Joyride game includes all the basic functionalities which are implemented almost in all types of 2D games such as side scrolling, parallax scrolling, sprite sheets, jumping, random obstacle generation, enemy generation, enemy Artificial Intelligence, particle systems, and animations.

Perky Penguin gameplay

The game features a penguin that is on ice in very cool (pun intended) and that's why she is called penguin. In order to navigate through an ice field in the time of global warming, she gets a hold of a jetpack, which is tied on her back. The game uses a simple, one-touch system to control the penguin; when the player presses anywhere on the touchscreen, the penguin's jetpack is fired and penguin rises above the ground making a feel like she is flying for a moment. When the player lets go, the jetpack turns off and penguin falls. The game is continuously running in side view, so player is not required to control the speed of penguin. The player is only able to control the vertical movement of penguin by turning the jetpack on and off.

The objective of the game is to travel as far as possible, collect fish coins, and avoid obstacles such as zappers, missiles, and high-intensity laser beams.

In the next section, we will start the development of the Perky Penguin game. We will learn how to add the player, which in our case is a penguin with jetpack tied to her back, to the game.

Adding the penguin

In this section, we will learn how to add our penguin player to the game and how we can make her alive by writing scripts, applying physics, and adding colliders in it.

Importing the penguin Sprite

Before we do anything, we need a player Sprite or image. For our Perky Penguin game, we have designed a penguin sprite. The following figure shows the penguin that is included as the player sprite of the game:

Figure 1.35 Penguin Sprite

To import an image in to Unity, right-click on the **Graphics** folder in the **Project Browser** panel and click on **Import New Asset...**, as shown in the following screenshot:

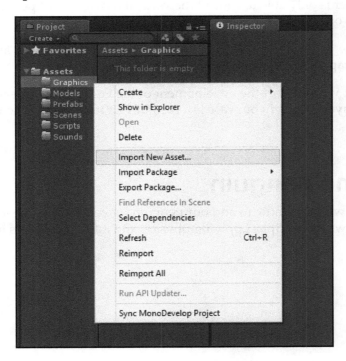

Figure 1.36 Import New Asset in Unity

These assets can be anything that is supported by Unity, such as images, audio files, 3D models, textures, materials, and scripts.

Assets can also be imported by dragging image files from Explorer to Unity's project browser panel.

Unity shows all the images with nice previews. It must be noted here that if Unity is in 2D mode, then unity will show images as sprites and if mode is set to 3D mode it shows the images as textures. *Figure 1.36* shows both scenarios. The following screenshot shows the image imported as sprite and the screenshot besides it shows image imported as texture:

Figure 1.37 Images as Sprites (left) and Images as Textures (right)

If the penguin image is imported as texture, then there is nothing to worry about. Select the image from **Project Browser** panel, and in the inspector change the **Texture Type** to **Sprite** and click Apply. It is shown in the following figure:

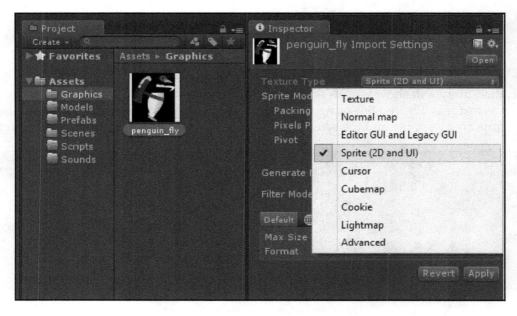

Figure 1.38 Change Texture Type of Image in Inspector Panel

Creating penguin game object

After the assets are imported, which in our case is a single penguin image, we have to create a game object of player. Usually game objects are created by right-clicking in **Hierarchy** and selecting **Create Empty** as shows in the following figure:

Figure 1.39 Creating Empty Game Object

But, in order to create sprites as game objects, simply drag sprites from the **Project Browser** panel to **Hierarchy** or **Scene View** panels and a game object will be created with the name of image file which is penguin_fly.png here. This is shown in the following figure:

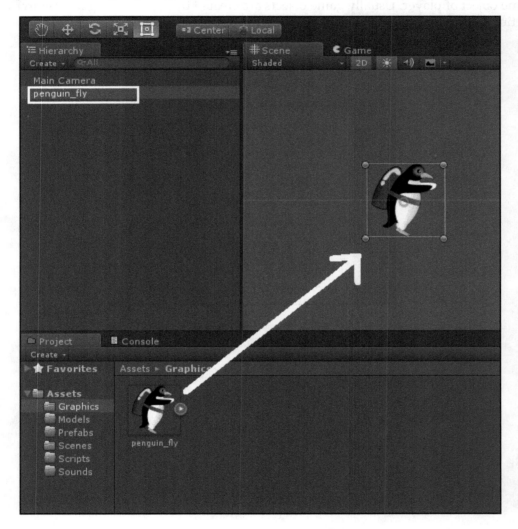

Figure 1.40 Creating Sprite Game Object

Now it's time to configure the **penguin_fly** game object of **Hierarchy** to get used in the game. Now select the **penguin_fly** object and make following changes in the **Inspector** panel.

1. Change the game object's name to `penguin`.
2. Set the position values to (0, 0, 0).

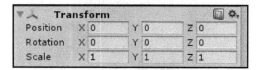

3. To add a collider in the penguin, click **Add Component** in the inspector and select **Circle Collider 2D** from **Physics2D** menu as shown in the following figure. More about Colliders can be read here `https://docs.unity3d.com/ScriptRefe rence/Collider.html`:

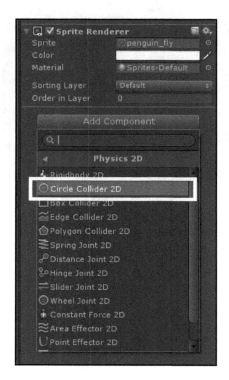

Figure 1.41 Adding Circle Collider 2D

4. Set the value of **Radius** of **Circle Collider 2D** to 0.6.

5. To make the penguin behave as a physical object, we have to add **Rigid Body** component. To add it, click **Add Component** in the Inspector panel and select **Rigid Body 2D** from **Physics2D** as shown in the following figure:

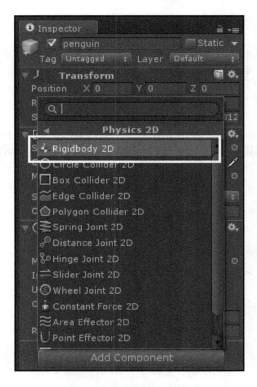

Figure 1.42 Adding Rigid Body 2D

6. Set **Fixed Angle** checkbox state as checked on to avoid penguin to be rotated while falling or jumping due to physics dynamics.

The following figure below shows all the steps performed on the penguin game object:

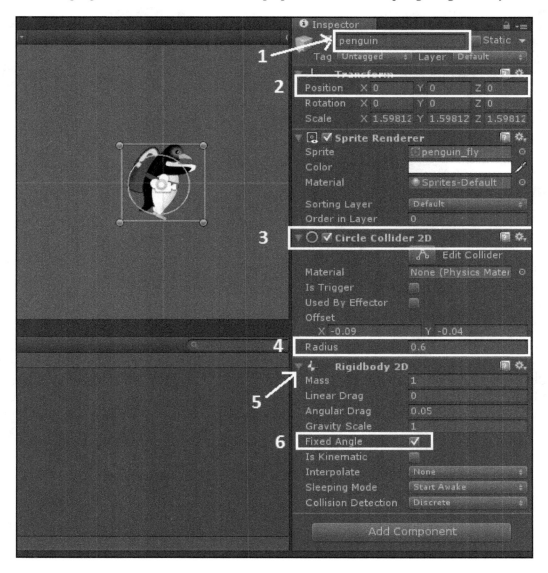

Figure 1.43 Penguin Inspector Settings

Starting from position, we have set the position to zero just for testing purposes. We will change it later when we put penguin at its initial position. The **Sprite Renderer** component is already added in the penguin game object because penguin game object was created from sprite by dragging it from **Project Browser** panel. The **Sprite Renderer** allows any game object to show an image on the screen from any sprite. In order to make any game object to react to physics collisions and get collided with each other, game object requires collider component in it. We have added **Circle Collider 2D** on the penguin object. You can choose any type of collider from the list. But it is recommended to choose the collider which is very light and fills the whole colliding area. The following figure shows the penguin with different colliders applied to it:

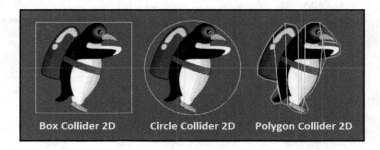

Figure 1.44 Penguins with Different Colliders

Using complex colliders like **Polygon Collider 2D** makes it harder to detect collision for the physics engine to detect collision, which in turn, creates a performance penalty. Finally, in order to apply gravity on the penguin, we have added **Rigid Body 2D** component. **Rigid Body 2D** allows any game objects to behave to the gravity, friction, physics kinematics and so on. We have check **Fixed Angle** to on state of the **Rigid Body 2D**. If this is set to off, then penguin will also rotate due to wind, friction, gravity, or any other force applied on it. So in order to avoid her to rotate while jumping, we have set **Fixed Angle** as checked.

 There are **Physics** components and **Physics2D** components. These both are very different in functionality and are used for very different purposes. You must be very careful when apply physics components on the game objects.

When you run the project, you will notice that penguin will fall down on the screen. It is because of the gravity is pulling penguin downwards and it goes off the screen. The **Gravity Scale** value, which is 1 by default, decides the gravity of the penguin. If we remove or disable **Rigid Body 2D** component, then penguin will never move. So, it must be noted that without rigid body no force and collision will be applied on the game object.

Adding script behavior on penguin object

After setting physics components and position on penguin object, it's time to define some logic behavior of the penguin. The game's requirements are to let penguin fly through its jetpack when screen is touched by player and penguin will fall when touch is stopped. These kinds of logic are defined in Unity through scripts. Unity supports 2 kinds of scripts; C# and JavaScript. You can use any of these scripts. Even you can also use few files in C# and few other files in JavaScript in the same project. Throughout this book, we will do all the scripting through C#.

1. We will start by creating a C# script file in Scripts folder in Assets by right-clicking on **Scripts** folder and choose **C# Script** from **Create** menu as shown in the following figure:

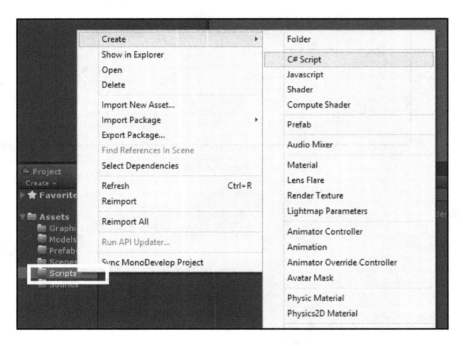

Figure 1.45 Adding a C# Script

2. Let's call this script as `PenguinController.cs` and when you open it, the Unity's default Code Editor **Visual Studio** will start and open the newly created script file it as shown in the following figure.

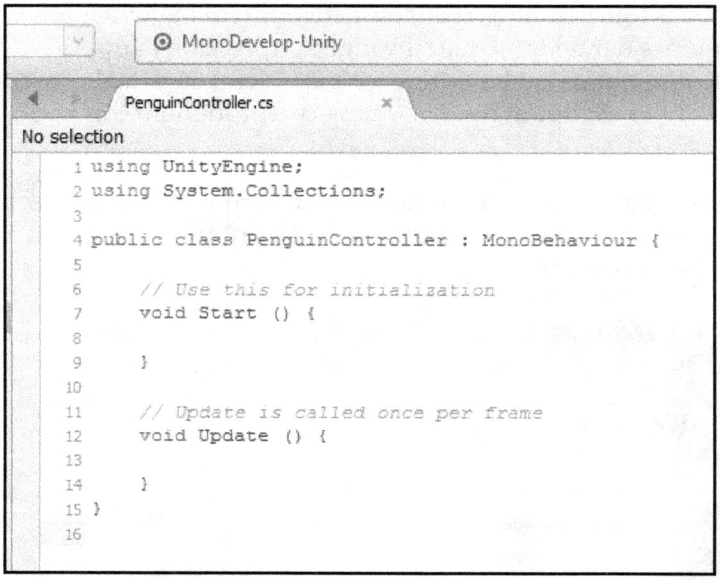

```
MonoDevelop-Unity

PenguinController.cs                    ×

No selection
 1 using UnityEngine;
 2 using System.Collections;
 3
 4 public class PenguinController : MonoBehaviour {
 5
 6     // Use this for initialization
 7     void Start () {
 8
 9     }
10
11     // Update is called once per frame
12     void Update () {
13
14     }
15 }
16
```

Figure 1.46 A C# Script File in MonoDevelop

3. You might notice some code already written in this file. We will discuss about it in a while. Now a script has been created, but this script is not linked or connected to our penguin object or even the game. In order to apply it on the penguin object, select **penguin** game object, click on **Add Component** in the **Inspector** panel, and choose **PenguinController.cs** from Scripts menu as shown in the following figure:

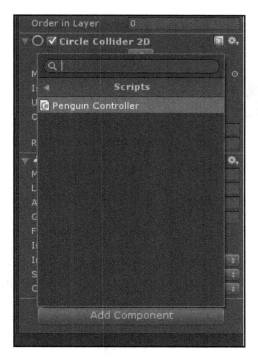

Figure 1.47 Adding C# Script on Penguin GameObject

 You can also apply script on the game object by directly dragging script file on the game object in hierarchy view.

Now, as the script is applied on the penguin game object, let's write some logic and code to make the penguin fly. Open `PenguinController.cs` file from project browser panel by double-clicking it in MonoDevelop. The code which is already written looks like the following screenshot:

```
1 using UnityEngine;
2 using System.Collections;
3
4 public class PenguinController : MonoBehaviour {
5
6     // Use this for initialization
7     void Start () {
8
9     }
10
11     // Update is called once per frame
12     void Update () {
13
14     }
15 }
16 |
```

4. The `PenguinController` class is inherited from `MonoBehaviour` class. Any script to be applied on any game object placed in the scene should be a `MonoBehaviour` class and this is done by inheriting the class from it. `MonoBehaviour` class provides some basic functionality for game objects such as its life cycle like when object is created, when it is active, when it is destroyed etc. Also it provides some functionality like interactions such as mouse down or mouse up etc. For now, we have only two methods `Start()` and `Update()`. The `Start()` method is called when the game object becomes first time active on the scene at runtime and `Update()` method is called on each frame if the game object is enabled or active.

You can also use Visual Studio 2012 with Unity for C# scripts by installing Visual Studio Unity Tools and importing UnityVS packaging in the project.

5. Now, let's start our logic for penguin. We will start from creating a variable `jetpackForce` in the class like this:

```
public float jetpackForce = 75.0f;
```

6. We have set its initial float value to 75 and f letter is to make it float literal. There is an interesting thing about Unity that all the public fields in any class will be shown in game object's inspector component and can be altered or modified directly from the editor without opening the code file. The following shows the `jetpackForce` variable's field in the inspector panel:

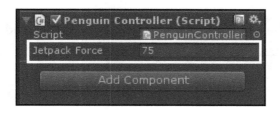

Figure 1.48 The jetpackForce Field in the Inspector Panel

7. Next is to use this `jetpackForce`'s value as the force to apply on penguin when touch is pressed. In order to detect touches, we have to use `Input.GetButton()` method. But this method is better used in either `Update()` or `FixedUpdate()` methods of `MonoBehaviour` class. The `FixedUpdate()` method is called every fixed frame instead of every frame. Meaning that in FixedUpdate() if the FPS of the game is 60 then the FixedUpdate function will be called 60 times in a second. Irrespective if there are any changes to the scene. In comparison the `Regular Update ()` function gets doesn't stick to the 60 fps rule and will update when there is a change in the scene. This should be used when dealing with **RigidBody**. As our penguin is a **RigidBody2D**, so it's better to use `FixedUpdate()` method than `Update()`. The `PenguinController.cs` script doesn't contain `FixedUpdate()` method, so let's add the following code in the class now:

```
void FixedUpdate()
{
    bool jetpackkActive = Input.GetButton ("Fire1");
    if (jetpackActive = true) {
        this.GetComponent<Rigidbody>().AddForce(new Vector2(0,
        jetpackForce));
    }
}
```

8. There is nothing difficult here. We are polling for the input of Fire1 button which is a left-click in case of any PC, Linux, or MAC build and it changes to touch on Android, iPhone or other touch device. If the screen is touched, then `GetButton()` will return true value, which in turn lets script add force by calling `AddForce()` method of the **RigidBody2D** component and passing the `jetpackForce` value in the y-direction.

Following is the whole `PenguinController.cs` file's code:

```
1 using UnityEngine;
2 using System.Collections;
3
4 public class PenguinController : MonoBehaviour {
5
6     public float jetpackForce = 75.0f;
7
8     // Use this for initialization
9     void Start () {
10
11     }
12
13     // Update is called once per frame
14     void Update () {
15
16     }
17
18     void FixedUpdate()
19     {
20         bool jetpackActive = Input.GetButton ("Fire1");
21         if (jetpackActive == true) {
22             this.GetComponent<Rigidbody2D>().AddForce(new Vector2(0, jetpackForce));
23         }
24     }
25 }
```

9. Now, when you run the game the penguin will start falling. On clicking on screen, the penguin will rise up a little and will start falling again. The more frequently clicks are performed, the higher penguin will go up and it will easily be out of the screen within 2 or 3 clicks. Also it is falling very fast. In order to adjust its speed, either we decrease **Gravity Scale** from **RigidBody2D** of the penguin object as shown in the following figure on left side or we decrease the **Gravity** in the **Physics2D** settings shown in the figure on right side.

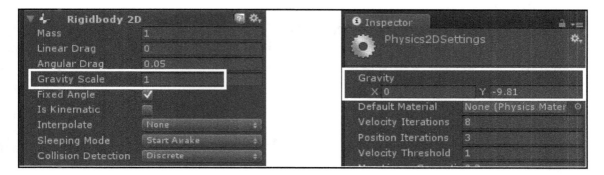

Figure 1.49 Gravity Scale of Penguin (left) and Gravity of Physics2D (right)

We will change the **Gravity** value of **Physics2D** settings to -15. You can open **Physics2D** settings from **Edit - Project Settings - Physics2D** menu.

Now run the game, and you will notice the penguin will fall slower than before. On clicking many times, you might notice that penguin gets out of the screen. This kind of behavior in the games should be avoided. So, in order to limit the penguin within the screen bounds, we will add floor and ceiling in the game. Let's see how it's done in the next section.

Limiting the penguin between screen bounds

Adding floor and ceiling is quite simpler job. We will create an empty object first. It should be noted that we are not importing any images or sprite assets in the scene, because we only need boundaries not the visuals of those about how these will look. Here is how we create our floor object.

- Create empty game object by choosing **GameObject - Create Empty** menu.
- Select newly created empty game object in the **Hierarchy** panel.
- Rename it to `floor`.

- Set its **Position** to (0, -3.25, 0).
- Set its **Scale** to (14.4, 1, 1).
- Add **Box Collider 2D** component by clicking on **Add Component**, and selecting **Physics2D - Box Collider 2D** option.

Now you should be seeing a green rectangle on bottom of screen. This is the box collider of the floor and when you run the game, the penguin will never fall off the screen and it will stop when collided with the floor.

 We haven't added **Rigid Body 2D** on floor object because we don't want to apply gravity on the floor object due to its static nature.

Similarly, now add ceiling game object with the name `ceiling` and its position of (0, 3.25, 0) and its scale of (14.4, 1, 1). Apply **Rigid Body 2D** component on the ceiling object, and now run the project. You will observe that penguin now never leaves the screen and it is limited between the upper and lower parts of the screen.

Summary

In this chapter, we learnt about what is Android and about its different versions. We also learnt about different game engines such as Unity3D, Unreal Engine, Game Maker Studio, or Adobe Flash used to create games for Android devices. We also learnt about important features of Unity along with its basics of its development environment. After learning basics of unity game development, we learnt about configuration of any empty game projects for 2D games. Then we got introduced to the Perky Penguin game which started getting developed in this chapter. A penguin was added and its basic flying and falling functionality was created in this chapter then.

In the next chapter, we will finish the Perky Penguin game and see how particle systems, animations, enemies, and so on, are all developed in Unity.

2
Finishing the Perky Penguin 2D Game

The previous chapter was all about new and beginner developers interested in Unity and game development. As this book is focused on game development for the Android platform, so the previous chapter, which happens to be the very first chapter of the book, introduced the Android platform, its different versions, and its marketplace, Google Play. Then the chapter revised the concepts of game engines and then brought Unity 3D into light by comparing it with other major game engines such as Unreal, Adobe Flash, and Game Maker Studio. The chapter made a transition through the very basics of Unity game development, such as introducing Unity's interface, its panels, such as the inspector panel, the hierarchy panel, and so on. It also introduced the concepts of scene view and game view and how they interact with each other and how these views help developers to make it an easy and fun experience to create awesome games.

This chapter includes the following topics:

- Adding particle systems to a game
- Camera management
- Prefabs and level management
- Lasers and enemies in a game

After providing enough information on the theoretical side of unity game development for Android platforms, the previous chapter started practical examples from configuring empty game projects which are especially useful for 2D games. Configuring empty projects is the very first step in any game and we covered this in Chapter 1, *Introduction to Android Game Development with Unity 3D*, in a very practical manner, and we also introduced a 2D game called **Perky Penguin**. The following is the screenshot of the game from the previous chapter:

Figure 2.1 Perky Penguin game

We learned how a player, such as the penguin, is added in Unity and how the colliders and physics were applied on the penguin. Unity also supports scripting and programming in C# or JavaScript languages to define custom behaviors such as making the penguin jump, avoiding gravity while flying, stopping the penguin from leaving the screen during gameplay, and so on. The chapter finished by having a Perky Penguin game with a penguin jumping in it.

If you are already familiar with the 2D concepts of Unity or have created 2D games already, then you can skip this chapter and move on to the third dimension.

In this chapter, we will finish this Penguin Perky game by learning some other advanced concepts of Unity 2D, such as adding particle effects, camera management, creating levels, using animations and controllers introduced in Unity 4.x versions, and so on. Until now, the Perky Penguin game has a cute penguin that can fly and jump on the screen but it can't walk forward and neither can it explore the game world. One thing to note here is that how the penguin is flying, whereas in real life, penguins don't fly. In our game, the penguin has got its hands on a red rocket which gives a boost of fire on the penguin to make it fly for a little instant. In the game, this boost is applied by a single tap on the screen of an Android device.

In the next section, we will start work on our game and bring the game to life by adding particle effects.

Adding Particle Systems

Before we delve into the details of particle systems, let's discuss what exactly these systems are and how they are used. Let's start with a discussion of what particle systems are.

What is a Particle System?

In any 3D complex game, characters, props, and environment elements are mostly created as 3D meshes and models, while in 2D games, sprites and images are used for these same purposes. Now, whether these objects are meshes or sprites, they mostly represent solid objects which contain a well-defined shape. But any game contains other entities such as fluids, liquids, smokes, clouds, flames, magic balls, and so on. These are some sort of special kinds of animations and objects, and are handled also with a special type of properties and behaviors, called particle systems in Unity.

The screenshot below shows some interesting magic spell particle systems created in Unity:

Figure 2.2: Different Particle Effects or magic spells created in Unity

Particles are small and simple images, or even meshes, that are displayed and animated in a huge number by a full-fledged system known as a Particle System. In any particle system, each small particle contributes a minor role and, overall, it looks like some highly polished animation or effect. For example, a snowfall effect can be treated as a particle system. A single particle of snow doesn't represent any snowfall if it is animated singularly, but if those same single snow particles are animated in a huge quantity with random speed, random direction, and random size, all these particles will not look like some image animation; rather, they will look like a system of snowfall in the game. That's the main key power of using a Particle System in Unity--it allows batch operations of heavy code in a very light and optimized way, resulting in very beautiful effects for games.

Basics of Particle System

In Unity, a Particle System consists of all of the particles. Developers are only expected to manage the particles and the rest will be handled by Unity. Each particle has a predetermined lifetime through various changes, such as fading away for any snowfall effect, or getting scaled up and fading for any smoke effect, and so on. Like all other physical game objects, these particles have velocity to change the speed and direction throughout their lifetime duration, and these particles can be affected by forces and gravity applied by the environment's physics kinematics.

The developers' end is to manage and control the particle's lifetime and its behavior, such as how many seconds will a particle last? How it will grow throughout its lifetime duration? Will it scale up or not? Will it fade away throughout its lifetime? All these questions are answered by developers and Unity will award them an amazing particle system in the form of an effect.

 The particles can be as simple as a sphere of white color or can be as complex as any mesh with high-resolution texture and normal maps.

The particle system's job is to manage all these particles from an abstract view. This system tells when to generate the next particle and where it should be, with what position, rotation, and scale. What should be the emission shape of the system, for example, hemisphere, code, or simple box? What should be the emission rate of the particles and how long should any particle effect take to execute one complete cycle of the system?

Creating a rocket fire Particle Effect for a game

So, after getting to grips with some basic knowledge of particle effects and particle systems in Unity, let's put this knowledge into action by creating the first particle system for our Perky Penguin game. As we know, the penguin wears a rocket tied to its back which lets it fly and boost when tapped on screen by the player. Now, this rocket will create a small fire-like effect when it becomes active. The following screenshot shows the rocket with its fire effect of boost as the final result of this small particle system exercise:

Figure 2.3: Rocket's fire effect final result

As shown in the preceding screenshot, you can observe how the fire starts from the edge of the rocket and how it disappears slowly with a fading effect, similar to real life. Now, let's create this simple particle effect for our penguin's rocket in our last created PerkyPenguin_PenguinMovement project from Chapter 1, *Introduction to Android Game Development with Unity 3D*.

Let's start creating a particle system object by selecting **GameObject** | **Particle System** as shown in the following figure:

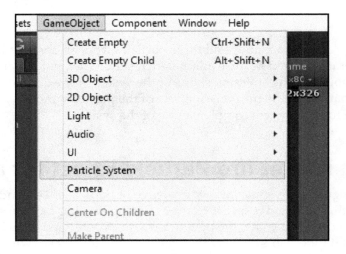

Figure 2.4 Creating Particle System GameObject

This will add a game object with the name **Particle System** in the **Hierarchy** panel immediately. But you might notice a strange thing here of the white spheres moving outward in the **Scene View** as soon the object is created and selected. The screenshot below shows a simple example of those white spheres in the Scene view below:

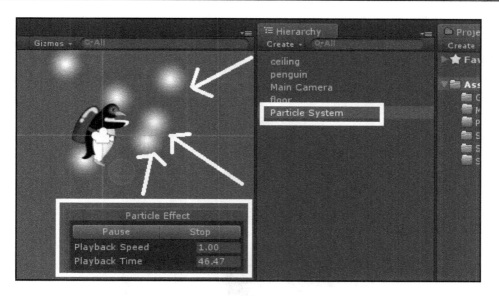

Figure 2.5 A Particle System GameObject selected in Unity

You can see that, as we created a Particle System object, a simple white sphere particle system started playing in the scene. A small control panel is shown in the scene, consisting of controls such as pause, stop, playback speed, and playback time. As you select any other game object or deselect the Particle System game object, the Particle System will stop automatically.

 One of feature of the interface of Unity is that developers don't need to play the game in order to test their particle systems. These can be checked directly within the scene view.

Also, you should notice the **Inspector** panel of the selected Particle System and see how lots of different properties are shown in the **Particle System** component of the object, as shown in the following screenshot:

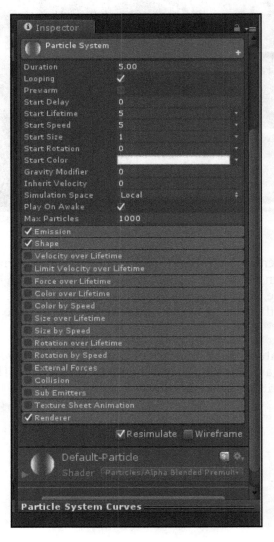

Figure 2.6 Particle System component in Inspector panel

It would be good to know that almost everything about the Unity's Particle System is provided in this **Particle System** component, which is a set of a huge number of properties. On tweaking and changing the values of these properties, a snowfall can be converted into burning fire, or it can be converted into an explosion for any airplane games, or it can be converted in a magic ball or magic spell for any dungeon role-playing games, and so on. To learn about it, let's continue our rocket fire particle system by following the steps given below:

- In order to put the particle system always below the rocket, it should be a child of the **penguin** object. So drag the **Particle System** object onto the **penguin** game object in the **Hierarchy panel** and you will see something like the following screenshot:

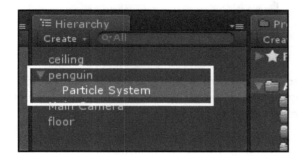

Figure 2.7 Particle System GameObject as child of penguin object

- Rename the **Particle System** to **rocketFire**.
- Set its **Position** to (-0.62, -0.33, 0) to move it to the nozzle of the rocket.
- Set its **Rotation** to (65, 270, 270) to set the direction of the particles in orientation with the rocket.

The following screenshot highlights all the changes provided in the above steps of the **Inspector** panel:

Figure 2.8 The rocketFire Transform in Inspector panel

Still in the **Inspector** panel with the **rocketFire** particle system object selected, let's alter the values of the **Particle System** component to create a beautiful type of fire for our penguin's rocket to boost. Here are the steps to follow:

- Set **Start Lifetime** to 0.5
- Set **Start Size** to 0.3
- Click on **Start Color** and set **Red** to 255, **Green** to 135, **Blue** to 40 and **Alpha** to 255, this will turn our white particles into orange ones
- Expand the **Emission** section and set **Rate** to 300
- Expand the **Shape** section and set **Shape** to **Cone**, **Angle** to 12 and **Radius** to 0.1
- Set the **Random Direction** checkbox to checked state to create randomness in fire particles

The following screenshot shows the **Particle System** component's previously set along with its result of rocket fire below the penguin in the **Scene view**:

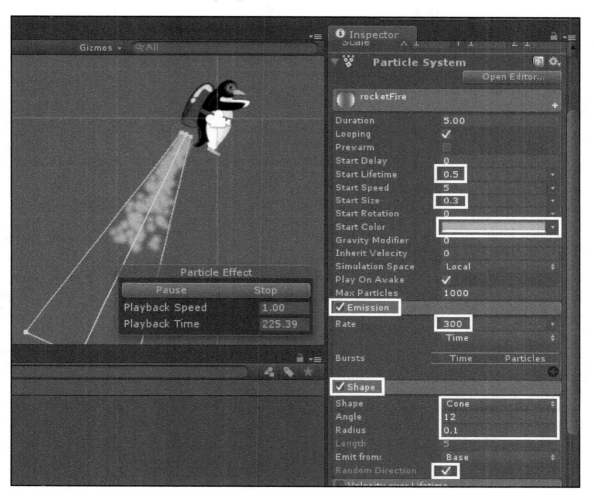

Figure 2.9 The rocketFire Particle System

You can observe how the random white spheres being generated and moving in random directions have changed into a cone-shaped fire emission from a rocket tied on the back of the penguin. What we have done is to alter some values in the Particle System component in the Inspector panel. Let's briefly look at what these properties actually do:

- **Start Lifetime** is the total lifetime in seconds that particles will have when emitted
- **Start Size** is the initial size of particles when emitted
- **Start Color** is the initial color of particles when emitted
- **Emission Rate** is the number of particles emitted per unit of time or distance moved
- **Shape** is the shape of the emission volume: the options are *Sphere, Hemisphere, Cone, Box, Mesh, Circle* and *Edge*
- **Angle** is the angle of the cone at its point (for cones only)
- **Radius** is the radius of the circular aspect of the shape
- **Random Direction** enabled means that the particles' initial direction will be chosen randomly

 You can see more of these properties and their purposes on Unity's manual or documentation website at `http://docs.unity3d.com/Manual/ParticleSystemModules.html`.

So, our rocket fire Particle System is ready. But, in real life, fire never ends instantly, it always ends by getting faded over time. We can also add this property into our fire by enabling the **Start Color** property in the **Particle System** component. Then click on the **Color** box and select the top slider on the right, which is for alpha of the end color, and set its value to 0.

The whole setting is shown in the following screenshot:

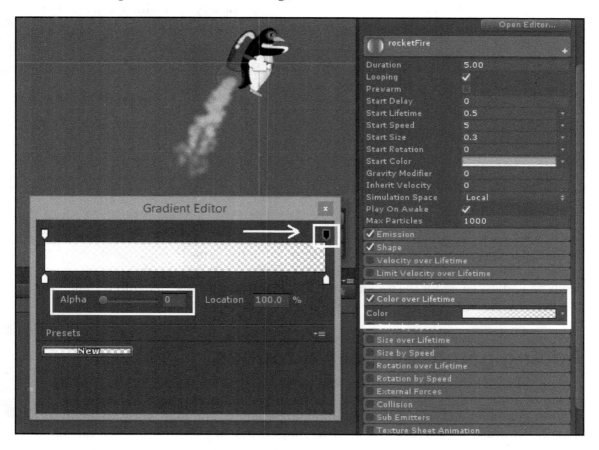

Figure 2.10 Adding fade effect in fire using Color over Lifetime

If you are not sure of what exactly **Color over Lifetime** changed in the fire effect, the following screenshot shows the difference in the fire particle system with and without the fading effect:

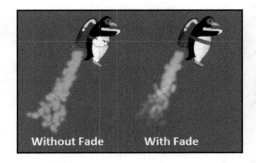

Figure 2.11 The fire effects with and without fade effects

So far, we have a penguin which flies on a tap of the screen and its rocket is exploding fire all the time. Now it's time to put some environment in the game to make the theme of the game. This environment will be for the penguin to move forward through and our game needs an endless room for the background. But, in order to test the penguin walking, we will only add background without any endless moving functionality.

Adding game-level backgrounds

A game with no background or theme is no game at all. So far, the penguin has got no reason to walk through the game, fly, or use its rocket to boost because it is in a void space of blue color. Let's bring this penguin into the snowy and hilly world where it actually belongs. And in order to survive melting ice due to global warming, it can also use its rocket to fly a little. In this section, we will learn how to add backgrounds and how the order of these backgrounds and sprites is managed in any 2D game where z-order is not used at all.

We will start by creating backgrounds for the levels of the game. These backgrounds can be created in your favorite graphics tools, such as Adobe Photoshop and so on. The following screenshot shows the background we created for the Perky Penguin game:

Fig 2.12 Background of the Penguin Perky Game

We have already learned about how the images are imported as sprites in Unity. For backgrounds, we have to do exactly the same procedure again. We have prepared two repeatable images with the names `bg_snow1.png` and `bg_snow2.png` and imported these images into the **Graphics** folder of the **Assets** directory in the **Project Browser** panel. The following screenshot shows the **Project Browser** panel with background images in it:

Figure 2.13 Backgrounds in the Project browser panel

It must be noted that the backgrounds should be repeatable so that when these images are put together, they should merge and avoid players recognizing the repeating order. The following screenshot shows both the background images we have designed for the Penguin Perky game:

Figure 2.14 Backgrounds of Penguin Perky game

You can see in the images that if we keep these two images repeating beside each other, it will create a very smooth background which will forever be repeating over and over again. We will do that with some scripting later in this chapter. For now, let's set up the scene background of the game.

After importing the background images in the **Graphics** folder of **Assets**, place two objects of bg_snow1.png and one object of bg_snow2.png in the **Hierarchy** panel. Set the first bg_snow1.png position to (0, 0, 0), then the bg_snow2.png position to (4.8, 0, 0), and finally another bg_snow1.png position to (9.6, 0, 0), and you will get a small background in the scene. So, now you will observe that the penguin is hidden behind these backgrounds. As this is a 2D game, so there is no concept of a z-axis here. We can set the z-axis position and bring forward and backward the sprites and images but for 2D games it is not a good approach. Unity provides developers with an ordering mechanism for placing 2D images front and backward optimized for 2D games especially. This is done through the sorting layers. Select the bg_snow1 object in the **Hierarchy** panel and look at the Inspector in the **SpriteRenderer** component, and you will see an option of **Sorting Layer** as shown in the following screenshot:

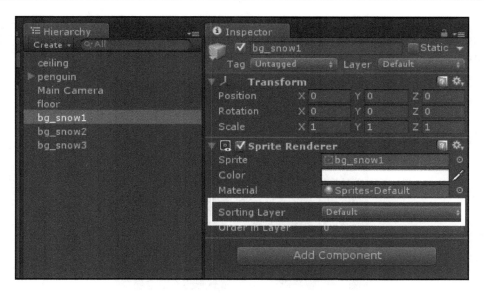

Figure 2.15 Sorting Layer in SpriteRenderer in Inspector panel

Initially, all the sprites you import in Unity have a default sorting layer. Click on the drop-down menu and you will see the list of all sorting layers in the project. At the moment, we only have one layer called **Default** and there is another option, **Add Sorting Layer...**, to add a new layer. Click on the **Add Sorting Layer...** option as shown in the following screenshot:

Figure 2.16 Add Sorting Layer... option

This will open a new **Tags & Layers** panel in place of the Inspector panel. Add four layers, namely Background, Surroundings, Objects, and Player in the order as explained. This is shown in the following screenshot:

Figure 2.17 Sorting Layers panel

You can drag these layers up or down by pressing and dragging the two lines icon to the left of each layer row. Moving these layers up or down describes the order of layers. For example, currently the Default layer is the lowest layer and it will be behind everything, and the Player layer will be in front of everything that uses layers except the Player layer.

There is a huge difference between **Sorting Layers** and **Layers**. **Sorting Layers** are only used to arrange 2D sprites for 2D games but the **Layers** are not for arranging purposes. It's totally a different concept and you must be careful when using layers in order to avoid any conflict between layers and sorting layers.

Right now, we only need Player and Background sorting layers; we will use other layers later in this chapter. Now, select the penguin game object in the Hierarchy panel and choose the Player layer from the Sorting Layer option in Sprite Renderer, as shown in the following screenshot:

Figure 2.18 Selecting Penguin's Sorting Layer

Similarly, select the Background layer for all the snow background objects in the scene. And now you will observe that the penguin will be in front of these snow backgrounds.

Camera management

So now we have a game in which we have a penguin that can fly and jump with a rocket fire particle system effect. Also, we have a basic environment of snow backgrounds in the scene as well. In this section, we will learn about how we to make the penguin move throughout an endless generated level and how the camera will always be focused on the penguin.

Making the penguin move forward

Let's start by making our penguin move in a forward direction. To do that, open the file `PenguinController.cs` created in `Chapter 1`, *Introduction to Android Game Development with Unity3D*. This file is contained in the **Scripts** folder of the **Assets** directory. Add the forward speed public field in the class, as shown in the following code:

```
public float forwardMovementSpeed = 3.0f;
```

Recall that adding any public field results in the addition of a property in the script's game object, as shown in the **Inspector** panel in the following screenshot:

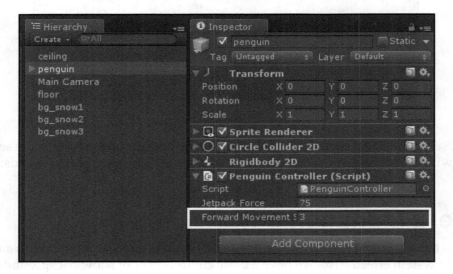

Figure 2.19 Forward Movement speed field in the Inspector panel

Now, in order to move the penguin with any speed, we have to update the speed of the penguin in the `Update()` or `FixedUpdate()` methods. Since we are using the `FixedUpdate()` method in order to utilize the physics behavior of the penguin, so add this code at end of the `FixedUpdate()` method:

```
// Velocity of Penguin
Vector2 newVelocity = this.GetComponent<Rigidbody2D> ().velocity;
newVelocity.x = forwardMovementSpeed;
this.GetComponent<Rigidbody2D> ().velocity = newVelocity;
```

Well, there is not much of anything new in this code snippet. As we updated the penguin's y-position in through jetpack force, we are updating only the x-axis of the penguin's object. See how we are assigning `forwardMovementSpeed` in each frame on the velocity of penguin's game object. When you run the project, the penguin will start moving in the right direction, and after a minute, it will leave the screen. Our next task is to make the camera follow the penguin so that the penguin always remains on screen and never gets out of bounds of the camera.

Making the camera follow the Penguin

Object as a child of the penguin game object, as shown in the following screenshot:

We have lots of methods to make the camera follow the penguin. The easiest is to put the Camera object as a child of the penguin game object, as shown in the following screenshot:

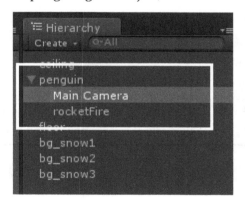

Figure 2.21 Camera as child of the Penguin object

Well, you can do this, but there is a problem with this solution. When the penguin jumps or flies, the camera also moves up or down with it. We don't need that in our game. We only need to move the camera horizontally and continuously move forward keeping the penguin in the bounds. So, we will do that by creating another C# script file in the **Script** folder of the **Assets** directory with the name CameraFollow.cs. Now, add a public GameObject field with a variable named targetObject. This field will tell the camera about which object to follow. We will keep a reference of the penguin's game object in this field. And finally, to move the camera continuously forward, we will do code similar to the penguin's moving forward code. The only difference here is that we put our code in the Update() method instead of FixedUpdate(). The reason for this is that FixedUpdate() should be used when the object has a rigid body and/or other physical behaviors. As our camera has no connection with the physics, we can do this by simply adding the moving code in the Update() method. The following is the whole code of the CameraFollow.cs file:

```csharp
public class CameraFollow : MonoBehaviour {

    public GameObject targetObject;
    private float distanceToTarget;

    // Use this for initialization
    void Start () {
        distanceToTarget = transform.position.x - targetObject.transform.position.x;
    }

    // Update is called once per frame
    void Update () {
        float targetObjectX = targetObject.transform.position.x;

        Vector3 newCameraPosition = transform.position;
        newCameraPosition.x = targetObjectX + distanceToTarget;
        transform.position = newCameraPosition;
    }
}
```

After writing the code, let's put this script on the **Camera** object. Select the **Main Camera** object in the **Hierarchy** panel, and click on the **Add Component** button in **Inspector** and choose **Scripts - CameraFollow.cs**, as shown in the following screenshot:

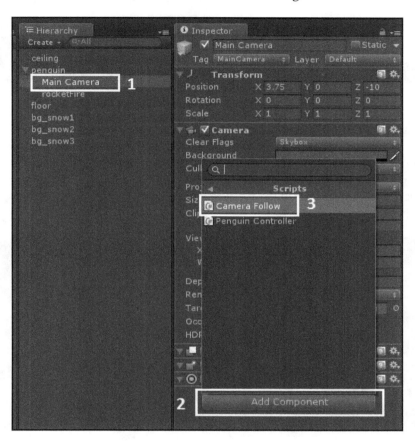

Figure 2.22 Adding CameraFollow.cs on camera

You can also apply scripts on the game objects by simply dragging the script files from the Project Browser panel directly onto game objects in the Hierarchy panel.

When you run the project, although the **Camera** will move, you will a see an error in the **Debug Log** panel, as shown in the following screenshot:

Figure 2.23 Camera error in Debug Log

The problem is that the variable `targetObject` in the `CameraFollow` script is not assigned to any value and we are accessing it the `Update()` method. Recall from earlier that we need to assign the penguin game object in the `targetObject` value to tell the camera about the target to follow. You can use Unity's public inspector feature and directly assign the penguin object by dragging it into the camera's `targetObject` field in the **Inspector** panel, as shown in the following screenshot:

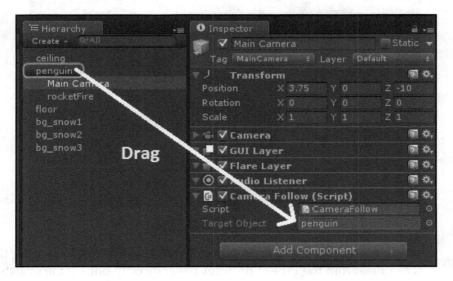

Figure 2.24 Assigning Penguin Object in Target Object

Now run the game and you will see the camera will never allow the penguin off the screen. However, after moving for a short time, the penguin will start falling since its floor has been left behind and the penguin has no physical support to oppose its gravity. To fix this and continue with the game, we will now work on creating endless levels in the next section.

Prefabs and level management

There is not a single game which doesn't contain at least one level. Levels are what makes games feel like an experience and adventure. Levels come with different kinds of difficulties and players start to have feelings of accomplishing something and rewards. So, to put the soul in our Penguin Perky game, let's add levels to our game. But the question that arises here is what type of levels we should add to the game. Since the game is endless, so it would be a very suitable to add automatically generated levels with random obstacles and enemies in the game. In order to do that, we need a script that will take care of generating random environments and rooms along with putting enemies and barriers to balance the game difficulty.

Unity provides developers with the opportunity to instantiate the game objects at runtime and define behaviours in them, also at runtime. We can add rooms, levels, coins, enemies, and so on separately at runtime but Unity provides a better and organized way to handle these types of situations to manage reusable elements at runtime. This is done through the Prefab objects. Let's discuss Prefabs in the next section.

Prefabs

According to Unity's documentation, a Prefab is a type of asset--a reusable `GameObject` stored in **Project View**. Prefabs can be inserted into any number of scenes, multiple times per scene. When you add a Prefab to a scene, you create an instance of it. All Prefab instances are linked to the original Prefab and are essentially clones of it. No matter how many instances exist in your project, when you make any changes to the Prefab, you will see the change applied to all instances.

The following screenshot shows the empty Prefab in the Project browser view:

Figure 2.25 An empty BoxPrefab in the Project browser panel

You will notice that we have a folder called Prefabs in our Assets directory. We created this folder when configuring the project. We will store all the Prefabs used in the game in this directory.

Prefabs are exactly like game objects. They can have colliders, rigid body, scripts, other components, and so on. The only difference between Prefabs and game objects is that Prefabs can be instantiated at runtime and copy the same behavior at runtime, but game objects can be generated at runtime.

In order to create an endless level, we have to create a small block of levels for our game. This block will be continuously generated at runtime over and over again as the penguin keeps going through the level. Let's create the small level block in the next section and see how this Prefab theory goes into action.

Creating a Level Block Prefab

The Level Block Prefab will have a ground object and a ceiling object to avoid the penguin going out of the bounds from the screen and it will have an environment in the background for decoration and theme purposes.

Let's start by creating an empty game object in the **Hierarchy** by right-clicking in hierarchy view and clicking **Create Empty**, as shown in the following screenshot:

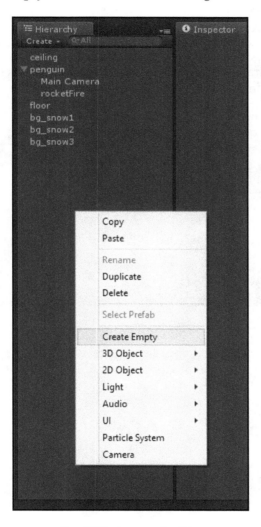

Figure 2.26 Creating an empty GameObject

Now, put all the necessary game objects to be included in the Prefab as a child of this empty game object. We are adding `snow_bg1` and `snow_bg2` backgrounds, the `floor` object, and the `ceiling` object at the moment. We can update it later at any time and add new objects and components in the Prefabs. But you must remember that it would change all the existing Prefab objects as well, so you must be careful when you update the Prefab.

All these objects can be dragged onto the empty created game object to make these children and rename the empty game object `level_block` then. The following screenshot shows the game object hierarchy of the `level_block` object:

Figure 2.27 The level_block game object

 If you have decorated your level block with more objects, decorations, surroundings, and so on, then you should also add them to the level block empty game object.

We have created a level block game object. Now it's time to put it into Prefab form. To do that, right-click on the **Prefabs** folder in the **Assets** directory, and choose **Create - Prefab** from the menu, as shown in the following screenshot:

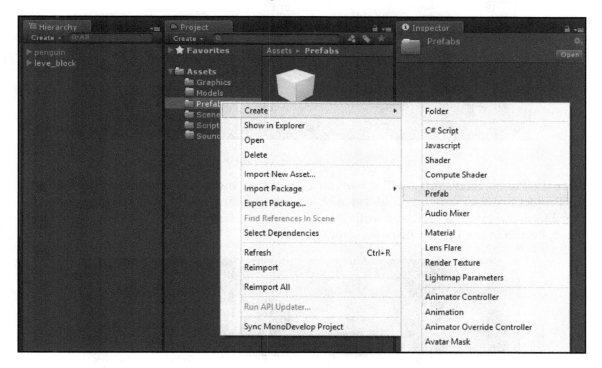

Figure 2.28 Creating a Prefab

It will create an empty Prefab in the **Prefabs** folder. Now, drag the **level_block** game object from the hierarchy view onto the empty created Prefab and your Prefab will be ready. This is shown in the following screenshot:

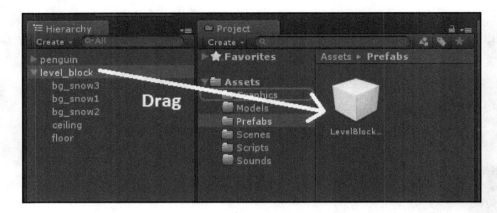

Figure 2.29 Adding an Object to a Prefab

Once the Prefab is created, it will show you a small preview of the game object contents in the **Project Browser** panel. You will also observe a small arrow in it, which will explore all the objects put into the Prefab as well. The following screenshot shows the preview of **Level Block Prefab** in the **Project Browser** panel:

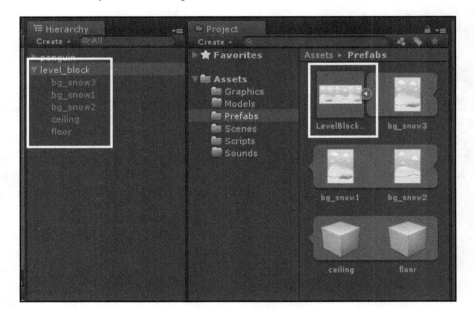

Figure 2.30 Prefab in Project Browser Panel

The Prefabs can be used in any scenes. These are reusable anywhere throughout the project.

In order to see how the Prefabs will work at runtime, just drag our Level Block Prefab object into the scene a few times in different positions and see how it comes in the view. The following screenshot shows a few level blocks placed in a scene:

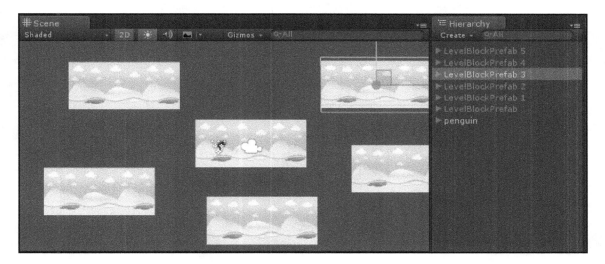

Figure 2.31 Level Block Prefabs placed randomly in the scene

You can observe that whenever we drag any Prefab into the scene, it creates the whole block, consisting of all the functionality, child objects, behaviors, scripts, and so on. That is the main advantage of using Prefabs in Unity.

Our Level Block Prefab is ready. Now we have to tell Unity when to create the block at runtime and at what positions it should be instantiated. We will do this by adding a script called `BlockGenerator.cs` into the penguin object. Let's explain about this generator in the next section.

The level block generator concept

The idea behind the generator script is quite simple. The script has an array of level blocks it can generate (for now, we have only one block created), a list of blocks currently generated, and two additional methods. One method checks to see whether another block needs to be added and the other method actually adds a block.

To check whether a block needs to be added, the script will enumerate all existing rooms and see whether there is a room ahead, farther than the screen width, to guarantee that the player never sees the end of the level. To understand this more clearly, let's look at the following screenshot:

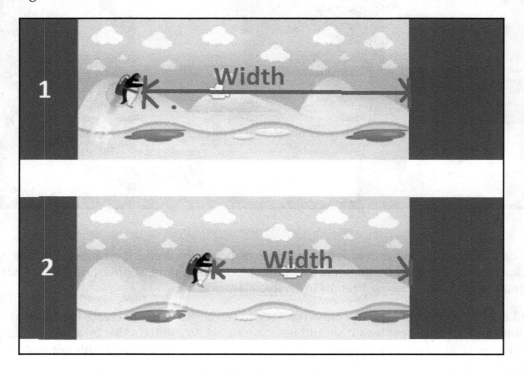

Figure 2.32 Level block generator idea

You can see in scenario 1, there is enough space or width yet to cover some distance in the block. But in scenario 2, there is not enough space to cover, because as the penguin moves forward, the empty space will start to show up. So before it shows any blank space, we need to add a new level block beside the current block so that the player never sees any empty spaces there. The figure only tries to clarify the rough concept of how the new block will be added and when. The following screenshot shows a sample generation of blocks and our penguin's moving forward status:

Figure 2.33 Penguin Moving Forward and Level Blocks Generating

You can see that as the penguin keeps moving forward, new blocks will be generating over and over again. Once any block leaves the screen, it will be deleted to optimize the memory usage and increase game performance.

Let's now bring this whole scenario into action by writing the `BlockGenerator.cs` code in the next section.

The BlockGenerator.cs code

Let's start by creating an empty C# script file in the Scripts folder of the Assets directory with the name `BlockGenerator.cs`. Then drag this script onto the penguin object to apply on the penguin.

 Any game object can have many scripts applied to it. There is no restriction of scripts or components applied on the game objects.

Open `BlockGenerator.cs` in `MonoDevelop` by double-clicking it in the **Project** view or in the **Inspector** panel.

 You have to add the `System.Collections.Generic` namespace if you're going to use the `List<T>` class.

Add the following field variables into the `BlockGenerator` class:

```
public GameObject[] availableBlocks;
public List<GameObject> currentBlocks;
private float screenWidthInPoints;
```

`availableBlocks` will contain an array of Prefabs which the script can generate. Currently, we have only one Prefab (`LevelBlockPrefab`). But we can create many different blocks types and add them all to this array, so that the script could randomly choose which block type to generate. The `currentBlocks` list will store instanced blocks, so that it can check where the last block ends and whether it needs to add more blocks. Once the block is behind the player character, it will remove it as well. The `screenWidthInPoints` variable is just required to cache screen size in points.

You can see these fields in the **Inspector** view of the penguin game object, as shown in the following screenshot:

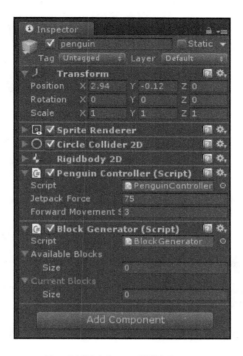

Figure 2.34 Block Generator Fields in Inspector

Now, add the following code in the Start() method of the BlockGenerator.cs file:

```
// Use this for initialization
void Start () {
    float height = 2.0f * Camera.main.orthographicSize;
    screenWidthInPoints = height * Camera.main.aspect;
}
```

Here you calculate the size of the screen in points. The screen size will be used to determine whether you need to generate a new block, described previously.

Add the following `AddBlock()` method to `BlockGenerator.cs`:

```
void AddBlock(float farhtestBlockEndX)
{
    //1
    int randomBlockIndex = Random.Range(0, availableBlocks.Length);

    //2
    GameObject room = (GameObject)Instantiate(availableBlocks[randomBlockIndex]);

    //3
    float roomWidth = room.transform.FindChild("floor").localScale.x;

    //4
    float roomCenter = farhtestBlockEndX + roomWidth * 0.5f;

    //5
    room.transform.position = new Vector3(roomCenter, 0, 0);

    //6
    currentBlocks.Add(room);
}
```

This method adds a new block using the `farhtestBlockEndX` point, which is the rightmost point of the level so far. Here is description of every line of this method:

- Picks a random index of the block type (Prefab) to generate.
- Creates a block object from the array of available blocks using the random index above.
- Since the block is empty containing all the block parts, you cannot simply take its size. Instead, you get the size of the floor inside the block, which is equal to the block's width.
- When you set the block position, you set the position of its center so you add the half block width to the position where the level ends. This way gets the point at which you should add the block, so that it starts straight after the last block.
- This sets the position of the block. You need to change only the x-coordinate since all blocks have the same y and z coordinates equal to zero.
- Finally, you add the block to the list of current blocks. It will be cleared in the next method, which is why you need to maintain this list.

After the `AddBlock()` method, let's go into the details of the
`GenerateBlockIfRequired()` method:

```
void GenerateBlockIfRequired()
{
    //1
    List<GameObject> blocksToRemove = new List<GameObject>();
    //2
    bool addBlocks = true;
    //3
    float playerX = transform.position.x;
    //4
    float removeBlockX = playerX - screenWidthInPoints;
    //5
    float addBlockX = playerX + screenWidthInPoints;
    //6
    float farthestBlockEndX = 0;

    foreach(var block in currentBlocks)
    {
        //7
        float BlockWidth = block.transform.FindChild("floor").localScale.x;
        float BlockStartX = block.transform.position.x - (roomWidth * 0.5f);
        float BlockEndX = BlockStartX + BlockWidth;
        //8
        if (BlockStartX > addBlockX)
            addBlocks = false;
        //9
        if (BlockEndX < removeBlockX)
            blocksToRemove.Add(block);
        //10
        farthestBlockEndX = Mathf.Max(farthestBlockEndX, BlockEndX);
    }
    //11
    foreach(var room in blocksToRemove)
    {
        currentBlocks.Remove(room);
        Destroy(room);
    }
    //12
    if (addBlocks)
        AddBlock(farthestBlockEndX);
}
```

This method is the implementation of the idea explained in the previous section:

1. Creates a new list to store blocks that need to be removed. Separate lists are
   required since you cannot remove items from the list while you are iterating
   through it.
2. This is a flag that shows whether you need to add more blocks. By default, it is
   set to true, but most of the time it will be set to false inside the `foreach`.

3. Saves player position.

4. This is the point after which the block should be removed. If a block's position is behind this point (to the left), it needs to be removed.

5. If there is no block after the `addBlockX`point, you need to add a block, since the end of the level is closer than the screen width.

6. In `farthestBlockEndX`, you store the point where the level currently ends. You will use this variable to add a new block if required, since the new block should start at that point to make the level seamless.

7. In `foreach`, you simply enumerate the current blocks. You use the floor to get the block width and calculate the `BlockStartX` (the point where the block starts, the leftmost point of the block) and `BlockEndX` (the point where the block ends, the rightmost point of the block).

8. If there is a block that starts after `addBlockX` then you don't need to add blocks right now. However, there is no `break` instruction here, since you still need to check whether this block needs to be removed.

9. If a block ends to the left of the `removeBlockX` point, then it is already off the screen and needs to be removed.

10. Here you simply find the rightmost point of the level. This will be the point where the level currently ends. It is used only if you need to add a block.

11. This removes blocks that are marked for removal. The mouse `GameObject` already flew through them and thus they are far behind, so you need to remove them.

12. If at this point `addBlocks` is still `true`, then the level end is near. `addBlocks` will be true if it didn't find a block starting farther than the screen width. This indicates that a new block needs to be added.

So, after all this explanation, let's add our final method, `FixedUpdate()` to the the `BlockGenerator.cs` files as follows:

```
void FixedUpdate()
{
    GenerateBlockIfRequired();
}
```

Generating blocks in `FixedUpdate()` will continue to periodically make sure that the player never experiences blank space in the game. Now, return to Unity and select the *penguin* GameObject in the Hierarchy. In the Inspector, find the `BlockGenerator` component. Drag the **LevelBlockPrefab** from the **Hierarchy** to the **Current Blocks** list. Then open the **Prefabs** folder in **Project Browser** and drag **LevelBlockPrefab** from it to **Available Blocks**. The following screenshot shows the `BlockGenerator` component of the penguin object after adding Prefabs in the lists:

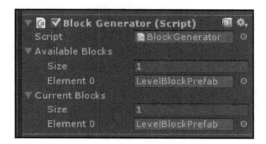

Figure 2.35 Block Generator Component with Prefabs

Now run the project and you will see that blocks will keep generating. Note that blocks are appearing and disappearing in the Hierarchy while you fly. And for even more fun, run the scene and switch to the *Scene View* without stopping the game. This way, you will see how blocks are added and removed in real time.

So, after level generation, let's discuss how to add obstacles such as ice spikes in the game to make the penguin be little careful while going through the level in the next section.

Adding ice spikes to the game

The penguin flying through the level looks great but the game is all about the challenges and obstacles. So, this section is all about the obstacles which can be added to the game. We will add ice spikes, which will be generated randomly in a similar manner as you generate blocks. Let's create the ice spike first. You need two images for the spikes on and spikes off states.

The following screenshot shows the spikes on and spikes off states:

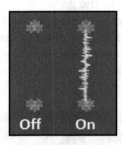

Figure 2.36 Block generator fields in Inspector pane

Import these images into Unity with the names `spike_on.png` and `spike_off.png` in the **Graphics** folder of the **Assets** directory. And then we have to create a Prefab of the spike for it. So, here are the steps below:

1. In the **Project** view, find the `spike_on` sprite and drag it to the scene.
2. Select it in the **Hierarchy** and rename it `spike`.
3. Set its **Sorting Layer** to **Objects**.
4. Add a **Box Collider 2D** component.
5. Enable the **Is Trigger** property in the **Box Collider 2D** component.

 When the Is Trigger property is enabled, the collider will trigger collision events, but will be ignored by the physics engine.

6. Set the **Size** of the collider, *X* to *0.18* and *Y* to *3.1*.
7. Create a new C# script named `SpikeScript.cs` in the **Scripts** folder and attach it to the `spike` game object.

The following screenshot shows all the steps done here to create a **spike** GameObject:

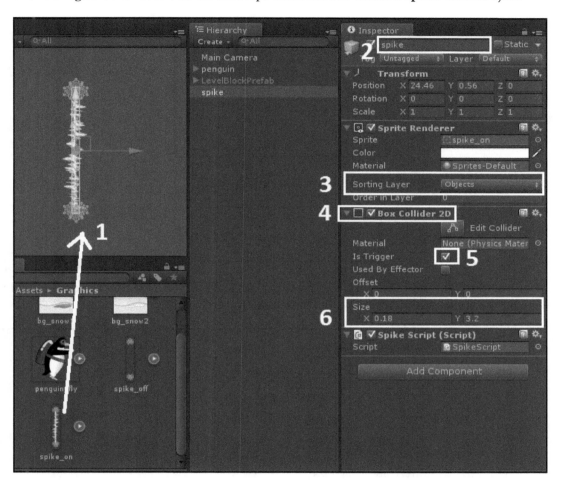

Fig 2.37 Adding a spike game object

Now open `SpikeScript.cs` and add the following fields in the class:

```
//1
public Sprite spikeOnSprite;
public Sprite spikeOffSprite;

//2
public float interval = 0.5f;
public float rotationSpeed = 0.0f;

//3
private bool isLaserOn = true;
private float timeUntilNextToggle;
```

Then add the following code in the `Start()` method like this:

```
// Use this for initialization
void Start () {
    timeUntilNextToggle = interval;
}
```

This will set the time until the spike should toggle its state for the first time. Then, to toggle and rotate the spike, add `FixedUpdate()` with the following:

```
void FixedUpdate () {
    timeUntilNextToggle -= Time.fixedDeltaTime;
    if (timeUntilNextToggle <= 0) {
        isSpikeOn = !isSpikeOn;
        GetComponent<Collider2D>().enabled = isSpikeOn;
        SpriteRenderer spriteRenderer = ((SpriteRenderer)this.GetComponent<Renderer>());
        if (isSpikeOn)
            spriteRenderer.sprite = spikeOnSprite;
        else
            spriteRenderer.sprite = spikeOffSprite;
        timeUntilNextToggle = interval;
    }
    transform.RotateAround(transform.position, Vector3.forward, rotationSpeed * Time. fixedDeltaTime);
}
```

Now, select `spike` in the Hierarchy. Drag the `spike_on` sprite from project browser to the Spike On Sprite property of the `SpikeScript` component in the inspector view. Also, do it for the `spike_off` sprite as well. Set Rotation speed to 30 and position to (2, 0.25, 0). Run the project and you will get a spike nicely rotating and finally turn into spike game object into a SpikePrefab in spikes folder as we did in the earlier section.

The following screenshot shows the spike running in the game:

Figure 2.38 Spike in the game

Summary

In this chapter, we continued our Perky Penguin game and added particle systems to it. Then we learned about managing the camera, and we made the camera follow the penguin throughout the game. Then we worked on Prefabs and created a level block Prefab which we generated in the game from the code to make an endless level generating game. Then we created a Spike Prefab to create an obstacle for the penguin in the game which gets generated randomly and rotates with different speeds at runtime.

In the next chapter, we will move our concepts of making games to 3D and introduce you to the workflow and systems to create 3D complex games in Unity 3D.

Summary

3
Adding Player Character for an Action Fighting Game

The previous chapter covered many different things and concepts regarding 2D game development in Unity and it followed a practical approach to finish a simple 2D game called Perky Penguin. The chapter continued the practice example of the game from Chapter 1, *Introduction to Android Game Development with Unity3D*, and finished by covering important topics on 2D games. It started by adding particle effects in Unity and then it explained in detail about the concept of Particle Systems, the basics of Particle Systems, and how these are added in Unity. Then we continued the discussion to apply the concepts in a practical example by adding a rocket fire particle system for the penguin in the game, and discussed such properties as emission, shape, and color.

After Particle Systems, the chapter focused on creating an environment and adding backgrounds in the game. It explained how to import these backgrounds, and how to make them repeatable in the game. The concept of sorting layers and tags was also covered and the chapter moved on to camera management and how a penguin would never go out of the screen if the camera always focused on it.

After these regular topics, a very interesting and useful topic of Prefabs was discussed in the chapter. After some basic discussion of Prefabs, the game was enlightened with Level Prefabs, which allowed the game to repeat the background and generate obstacles at runtime. This discussion also included the generator concept and its code implementation as well.

Finally, the chapter finished with adding obstacles in the game and the basic collision detection with the penguin. This led to the concept of triggers as well, which becomes very useful in creating invisible colliders to detect some object's presence at some place in the game. The following is a screenshot of the game after completion of the previous chapter:

Figure 3.1 A snapshot of Penguin Perky game

 If you are interested in creating any 2D game in Unity, then this is covered in more detail in Chapter 1, *Introduction to Android Game Development with Unity3D* and Chapter 2, *Finishing the Perky Penguin 2D Game.*

This chapter is a totally new level compared to previous chapters. In this chapter, we will extend our knowledge about Unity to 3D game development, which can often become very confusing and tricky for new game developers. Up until 2D game development, the focus of developers and programmers revolved around the concept of images, sprites, and two dimensions, ignoring the camera's depth. The new developers who have worked on graphics tools such as Adobe Photoshop or Gimp prove to be very good in 2D game development and grasp the concepts very quickly, but 3D becomes very tough because it needs expertise in highly-used advanced commercial tools such as Autodesk Maya, 3D Studio Max, and so on. These tools require many years of practice and experience and that makes 3D game development very hard to learn for new programmers.

It is out of the scope of this book to cover all the topics, but we will learn about basic concepts and their usage through creating a 3D action fighting game from scratch. This chapter will teach from the very start about the configuration of 3D game projects, importing 3D models, and how textures and materials are applied on these models. Moving on, this chapter will introduce the concept of rigging and what interfaces Unity has to offer to make rigging easier, such as humanoid rigging, generic rigging, and so on. This concept of rigging will be implemented in practice by importing and rigging the player character model of the action fighting game in Unity. We will further apply animations to allow for basic character movement.

Now, let's put our words into action and start learning about 3D game development, focusing on the configuration of 3D game projects in Unity in the following section.

This chapter includes the following topics:

- Configuring a project for 3D games
- Importing 3D models
- Applying textures and materials
- Generic and humanoid rigs
- Configuring humanoid avatars
- Legacy and Mecanim animation systems
- State machines with Animation controllers

Configuring Project for 3D Games in Unity

In previous chapters, we were learned about 2D games and we also learned about how 2D game projects are created and configured in Unity. For 3D projects, the procedure is almost identical, except some changes need to be done. Let's start by launching Unity 5 and creating an empty project with it.

If you are already aware of 3D game projects configuration or have worked on any 3D game before, you can safely skip this section. When you launch Unity 5, it shows a project wizard, as shown in the following screenshot:

Figure 3.2 Unity 5 new project wizard

The project wizard shows a list of all the recent projects along with their names. The most recent project is highlighted for quick opening. On the top-right side of the wizard, there are controls to create a new project from scratch and open any specific project from any directory. Let's start by creating a new project by clicking on the **New project** button on the top right. You will be presented with the dialog, shown in the following screenshot:

Figure 3.3 New project details wizard

Write the project name and select its path location. Below these text inputs, you will observe a simple selection from two options: 2D and 3D. We will choose 3D as we are creating a 3D game. This is shown in the following screenshot:

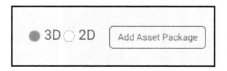

Figure 3.4 Project type selector for 2D and 3D

This toggle lets you tell Unity whether your project is 2D or 3D. Although this doesn't affect or change the project in any way while working on it, it affects the default project setting for an easier workflow. For example, in 3D mode when you import any image asset into the project, Unity will take it as a texture and in 2D mode, Unity will take it as a sprite. You can also change the mode later from the project anytime; it is not necessary to select at project creation time. By default, Unity will create the project in 3D mode.

Now, let's name the project as **Free Fighter** and press **Create Project**. This will import some pre-defined assets and launch the Unity interface editor. You can observe that an empty new scene will be created as well containing two game objects in the hierarchy panel: **Main Camera** and **Directional Light**. We won't discuss these objects at the moment, but these will be covered in upcoming chapters as we manage the cameras and lights for the games.

In this blank unsaved empty scene, the first thing we need is the model of the player character. Let's discuss the model or models in general in the next section.

Importing 3D models

Before we go into the nifty details of 3D modeling and Unity3D, let's discuss first what 3D models are. In computer graphics, 3D modeling is the process of constructing and developing a mathematical and visual representation of any three-dimensional (3D) surface of an object via any 3D modeling software. The end product of that process is called a **3D model**, or simply model, in the context of this book. The interesting thing about 3D models is that they are in 3D and any computer or laptop screen is a 2D surface, so it becomes a tricky task to display the 3D model in the horizons and bounds of 2D screens. So a process of displaying 3D models in the form of 2D images is used and this is called **3D rendering**. It comes with 3D software tools including our very own Unity3D. This rendering process uses lights and cameras to render the 3D model as it's something real and it presents the image of it in the viewer's mind. We can get into more and more details of this never-ending topic and discussion of 3D models but it is far outside the scope of this book. So, we will talk only about the important details that can help in building a 3D game in Unity, namely models and modeling tools.

3D modelling is the process of developing a mathematical representation of any three-dimensional surface of an object. Remember, a 3D model is the main asset of any game. A model file may contain a 3D model, such as any character, building, furniture, and so on. A model file may also contain animation data which can be used to animate this model or other models. The animation data is imported as one or more animation clips. We can't create 3D models in Unity because Unity is the gaming engine for developing games, not for creating 3D models. We just can just import them and use them in the game. There are many 3D modeling software packages available on the market, and they are improving day by day as well.

In Unity, importing meshes can be achieved from two main types of files: **exported** 3D file formats and **proprietary 3D application** files. Let's further describe exported 3D file formats. Unity can read .fbx, .dae, .3DS, .dxf, and .obj. The advantages and disadvantages of exported 3D file formats are described in the following text:

Advantages

- Only export the data you need
- Verifiable data (re-import into the 3D package before Unity)
- Generally smaller files
- Encourages modular approach; for example, different components for collision types or interactivity
- Supports other 3D packages whose proprietary formats we don't have direct support for

Disadvantages

- Can be a slower pipeline for prototyping and iterations
- Easier to lose track of versions between source (working file) and game data (for example, exported FBX)

The second type of files are the proprietary 3D application files such as .Max and .Blend file formats from 3D Studio Max or Blender. Unity also can import Max, Maya, Blender, Cinema4D, Modo, Lightwave, and Cheetah3D files. For example, MAX, MB, MA, and so on. The advantages and disadvantages of proprietary 3D application files are as follows:

Advantages:

- Quick iteration process (save the source file and Unity reimports)
- Simple initially

Disadvantages:

- A licensed copy of that software must be installed on all machines using the Unity project
- Files can become bloated with unnecessary data
- Big files can slow Unity updates
- Less validation, so it is harder to troubleshoot problems

3D models

3D models are the representation of any physical object constructed using a collection of geometric primitives such as triangles, lines, curved surfaces, and so on. The following figure shows some basic primitives used for the creation of 3D models:

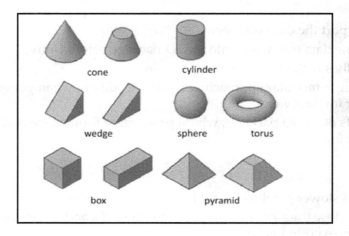

Figure 3.5 Some basic primitives for 3D modeling

All the 3D models and objects are created by assembling, modifying, nudging, and so on, these primitive shapes and objects. To understand it better, take a look at the following figure which shows some 2D primitives used behind the scenes of 2D graphics tools such as Photoshop or Gimp:

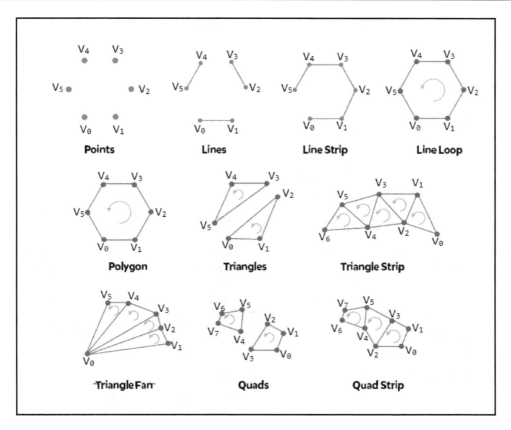

Figure 3.6 Some 2D primitives

Modelling tools

Now that you have a good understanding of 3D models, let's move ahead in our discussion with the modeling tools. These 3D models are created in very advanced and mostly commercial tools such as Autodesk Maya, Autodesk 3D Studio Max, Blender, and so on. These tools offer modelers a variety of choices and features to create and animate the 3D models and render them in the form of images or video movies, or directly export them into model files.

The following table shows some 3D modelling tools along with their license types of usage:

Tool name	License type
Autodesk Maya	Commercial
Autodesk 3D Studio Max	Commercial
Cinema 4D	Commercial
Cheetah 3D	Commercial
Blender	General public

Table 3.1 Some 3D modeling tools

Unity3D is not an advanced modeling tool but it offers some basic primitives and allows some basic modeling features as well. But, in order to create any 3D game or movie in Unity3D, you need more detailed 3D models in it. So, Unity3D allows developers and modelers to import most kinds of 3D model files to customize, animate, and use them in games or movies with programming as well. This feature makes Unity3D quite powerful indeed compared to other 2D or 3D game engines. Unity3D supports two types of files when it comes to import models:

1. Exported 3D file formats such as `.fbx`, `.dae`, `.obj`.
2. Proprietary 3D application/tool files or native files of modeling tools such as `.max`, or `.mb`.

The exported files tend to be lighter in size and these files allow you to select the data you want to use in Unity3D at the time of exporting it. Unity3D recommends these types of models to use in the game or movie in order to optimize it for the sake of real-time rendering and high performance.

The later proprietary files are the native source files of the models of tools such as Maya and 3D Studio Max. The biggest advantage of these files is that they allow for a quick iteration process of testing games/movies by seemingly re-importing models at the time of editing as well. But you need the licensed copy of the modeling tool on every computer in which you use Unity3D and the model files. These files are often very large and not recommended for releasing games or movies in Unity3D.

 It is highly recommended to use FBX files in Unity3D as it allows for embedding animations and textures directly in the model itself.

Importing 3D models in Unity3D

So, after a little detailed discussion on 3D models and modeling tools, let's get into the real details of how to import 3D models in Unity3D. If we say this in terms of importing sprites, images, and sounds, it sounds similar to putting any 3D model file in the `Assets` folder of the project, but it actually gets complicated due to lots of concepts and settings involved in the process of importing in Unity3D.

In this section, we will discuss how to import any 3D model in Unity. We will import a simple house model of FBX type in Unity now. The FBX type is short for Filmbox files and is used mostly in AutoCAD for CAD/CAM designing for houses, architectures, cars, and engineering modeling. Major 3D modeling tools also give the option of exporting models into `.fbx` format as well. The main advantage of using FBX files is that it allows developers to select which type of data should be exported in the file. This data can include meshes, mesh animations, rigs, or bone animations. We have used a simple house model as shown in the following figure, downloaded from The **Free 3D Models** (**t3fm**) website available for general public use:

Figure 3.7 A house model

Now, first open our 3D Free Fighter project in Unity, and you will see the **Assets** folder in the **Project** panel. Right-click on the **Assets** folder and create a new folder called `Models`. There are many methods of importing models into Unity3D. Click on the **Assets** menu and choose the **Import New Asset...** option and select the **Farmhouse.fbx** file and finally click on the **Import** button.

This whole process is as shown in the following screenshot:

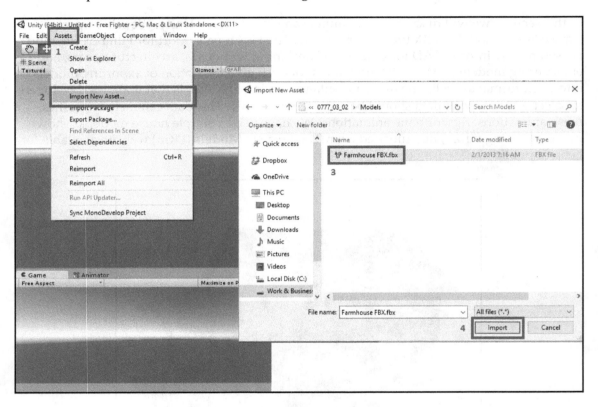

Figure 3.8 Importing 3D model in Unity3D

After importing, you will see that the file will be placed in the **Models** folder. But you will also notice that another folder with the name **Materials** will automatically be created with the model file in the **Project** panel, as shown in the following screenshot:

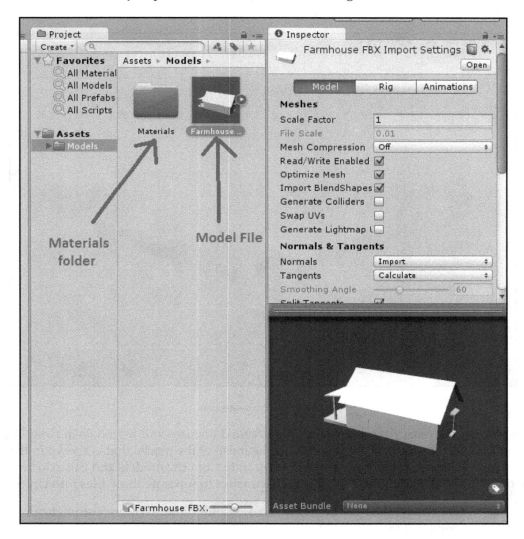

Figure 3.9 House model in project panel

Now the model is imported into Unity and it can be used in the game. You can drag it in the scene in a similar way as you did to add images and sprites in Unity3D. After dragging it into the scene, you will notice that the model is not colored. It's just a single color white and gray model as shown in the following screenshot:

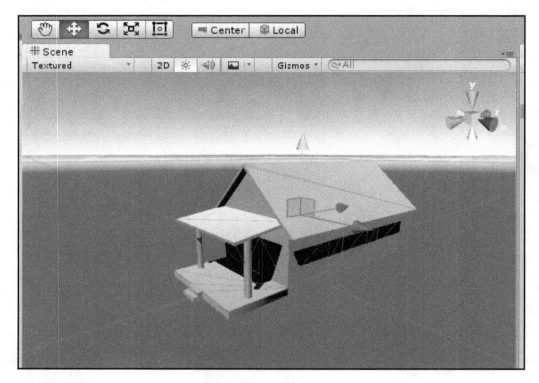

Figure 3.10 The house model in scene

The reason for the disappearance of the colors, called textures and materials in Unity3D, is that the .FBX file of this model only contains the mesh of the model that is shown in the scene. The textures and materials also come separate from the models and can also be embedded into the model file itself. It is good practice to separate these files into Unity3D.

The model files placed in the Assets folder manually are automatically imported into Unity3D.

A model file can contain any 3D model such as any character, building, or any geometric shape. We have a farmhouse model imported in Unity3D. In the **Scene view** or **Hierarchy** panel, the imported model is placed as a game object of the model prefab, which is automatically created by Unity3D at the time of importing the models. This game object will contain all the model data such as mesh, lights, and so on, as the children objects of it. The following figure shows the farmhouse model's game object in the **Hierarchy** panel:

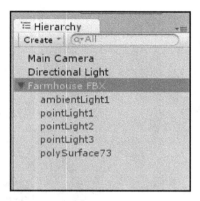

Figure 3.11 The Farmhouse model prefab object hierarchy

Developers often get confused after importing models with the different issues involved in the process. Some models become too much small in size after importing, or some models come rotated reversely in Unity3D. This is all about the settings of the model. Since these models are created in other tools such as Maya3D, the difference in scaling and scene settings can cause such issues.

So, in order to customize these settings more, Unity provides the properties of the model in the **Inspector** panel, which can help in setting the properties of the model before using it in the scene. When you select the imported model in the Assets directory, you will see some other settings in the **Inspector** panel, as shown in the following screenshot:

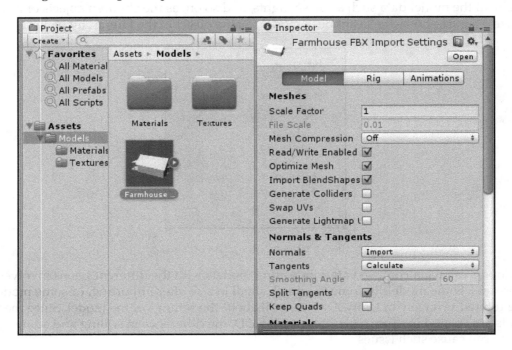

Figure 3.12 Farmhouse model settings

As you can see in the preceding screenshot, a model file contain three kinds of data presented in tabs form in the settings: **Model**, **Rig**, and **Animations**. The **Model** tab includes all the data related to the mesh, materials, and the model itself. The **Rig** tab and **Animations** tab allow developers to set the animation behavior of the model, either with the embedded animations in the model file itself or from other animation clips in Unity3D. We will discuss these details later in this chapter. Although there are lots of settings in the **Model** tab itself, we will discuss only some of the important settings which are used generally when importing FBX models in Unity3D:

1. **Scale**: This scale factor is used for removing the gap between the units system in Unity3D and the units system in the modeling tool in which the model has been created. Unity3D generally refers to one unit of the scale factor as one meter. So, developers should set the scale factor accordingly. Normally, this is set to 1.

2. **Generate colliders**: This check allows developers to automatically generate colliders for the mesh and model for the collision detection. Keep in mind that with this check enabled, Unity3D will create mesh colliders, which can sometimes result in very heavy processing, depending on the mesh itself. So, if you want the customized colliders, you can customize, or create your mesh collider in Unity as well.

These two settings will set the model to a good condition. We should be reminded that our model is still in a single color and we haven't yet imported textures and materials to it. So in the next section, we will discuss about applying textures and materials on the model objects.

 The default scale factor for different 3D models is as follows: `.fbx`, `.max`, `.jas`, `.c4d` = 0.01, `.mb`, `.ma`, `.lxo`, `.dxf`, `.blend`, `.dae` = 1, `.3ds` = 0.1.

Importing FBX Model

FBX is the abbreviation of Filmbox. Unity supports FBX files which can be generated from many popular 3D applications. Be aware of export scope, for example, meshes, cameras, lights, animation rigs, and so on:

1. Applications often let you export selected objects or a whole scene
2. Make sure you are exporting only the objects you want to use from your scene by either exporting selected data, or removing unwanted data from your scene.
3. Good working practice often means keeping a working file with all lights, guides, control rigs etc. but only exporting the data you need with export selected, an export preset, or even a custom scene exporter.

See the following figure to determine the difference between OBJ and FBX:

	Mash and Animations			
	Mash	**Mash Animation**	**Rig**	**Bone Animation**
OBJ	Yes	No	No	No
FBX	Yes	Yes	Yes	Yes

In Unity asset store, many 3d models are available free or paid, that can be easily used in any game. Also you can find on internet many website are available where user sell or royalty-free 3D models (`http://tf3dm.com`)

So, we have modelled a house in 3D Max, and exported it into FBX format; remember in that model we have only mash, do right click in the **Project** panel then click **Import New Asset...**, then browse you FBX model path and click **import** button. Unity provides us also with a drag and drop feature so we can drop an fbx model into the **Project** panel. The following figure shows how to import a model into the scene by clicking the **Import New Asset...** button:

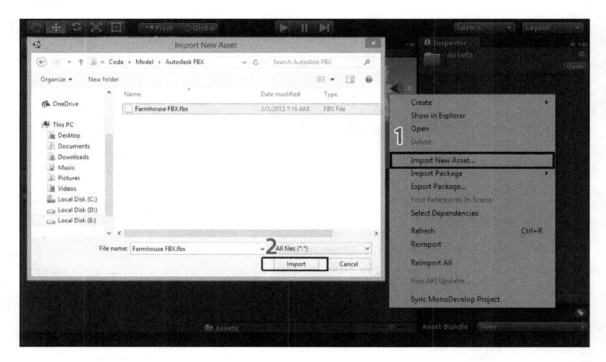

You can see the FBX model in the **Project** panel the better way to go forward your project in managed way so create empty folder name as **Model** in root, then drop your fbx file and material folder of it into the **Model** folder. The following figure depicts the drop FBX model into the **Model** folder:

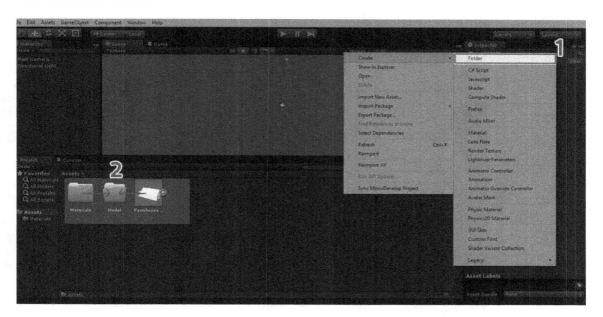

Now go to the **Model** folder and drag **Farmhouse FBX.fbx** file and drop it into the **Hierarchy** panel; if the models showing are small, that means the scale of models are small, to increase the scale size of model select **Farmhouse FBX.fbx** from the **Project** panel, you will see 3 tabs in **Inspector** panel named **Model**, **Rig** and **Animations**, we focus on model for now model are selected by default. In the first textbox, **Scale Factor**, do change value 1 to whatever you need let suppose 10, then click on **Apply** button end of **Model** panel.

Consider the following figure for illustrating the increase in the scale size of the model:

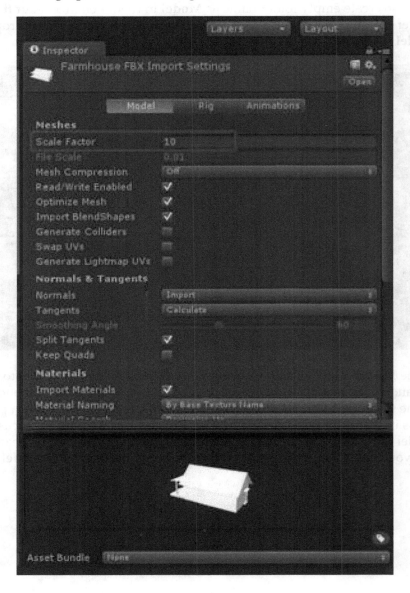

Applying textures and materials

When it comes to 3D modeling, textures and materials become tricky as they give life to models. The 3D modeling tools give quite a lot of flexibility to modelers and designers to work together and create amazing textures and convert them from simple images to 3D working models. Looking from a graphics and designing perspective, there are three components to materialize the model: textures, shaders, and materials. Unity3D gives lot of options to customize these three parts and lets developers create exactly what they want that model to look like. These three components are connected in such a way that developers can easily change and alter each component individually and see its results on the model in real-time. The following figure shows the connection of these three components:

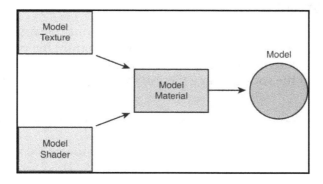

Figure 3.13 Connection between textures, shades, and materials

You can see in the preceding figure that textures are not directly applied on the model. Instead, they are applied on the materials and the materials are then applied on the model. Materials also add some materializing properties in order to behave with the lights present in the scene to make the model look 3D in the 2D world of the computer screen. Let's give a little detail to each component in the following sub-sections.

Textures

Generally, the mesh object gives a rough approximation of the shape of the model and how it will look like, but it's the textures that define the shape itself and present it in a real form from the perspective of the viewer. Textures are the flat bitmap images that are wrapped on the model mesh surface. The easiest example would be to think of them as the image that is printed on any 3D model, such as any cylinder or cube or any complex model such as our farmhouse.

The following figure shows this scenario:

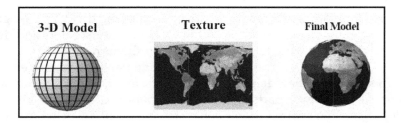

Figure 3.14 Texture on 3D model

Texture Importer

All the texture exist in the `Project` folder in the image form. Unity gives to change the type of texture--after importing a texture you just select texture from the project panel and modify from the topmost item in the inspector. That allows you to select the type of texture you want to create from the source image file. All the types of texture are shown in the following figure:

Property:		Function:
Texture Type		Select this to set basic parameters depending on the purpose of your texture.
	Texture	This is the most common setting used for all the textures in general.
	Normal Map	Select this to turn the color channels into a format suitable for real-time normal mapping. See the Details section at the end of the page.
	Editor GUI	Use this if your texture is going to be used on any HUD/GUI Controls.
	Sprite (2D and UI)	This must be selected if your texture will be used in a 2D game as a Sprite.
	Cubemap	Cubemap, often used to create reflections. See Cubemap Textures for more info.
	Cookie	This sets up your texture with the basic parameters used for the Cookies of your lights
	Advanced	Select this when you want to have specific parameters on your texture and you want to have total control over your texture.

Applying texture in shaders

The shaders you use for your objects put specific requirements on which textures you need, but the basic principle is that you can put any image file inside your project. If it meets the size requirements (specified in the following text), it will get imported and optimized.

There are certain steps to put texture in shaders:

1. After selecting **Model**, shaders will be visible in the **Inspector** panel.
2. **Texture** button is present in it, click on it for applying texture.
3. Select Texture, so that our 3D model will be wrapped in our selected texture.

This is represented in the following figure:

Unity can read the following file formats for texture PSD, TIFF, JPG, TGA, PNG, GIF, BMP, IFF, and PICT. It should be noted that Unity can import multi-layer PSD and TIFF files.

Shaders

In computer graphics, shaders are a little hard to understand for newbies. A texture tells the viewer of what is drawn on the surface and mesh of the 3D model object, but it is the shader that tells how that texture is drawn. As we saw earlier in *Figure 3.13*, a material is a mixture of textures and shaders. A material contains the properties and textures, and a shader tells us which properties and shaders a material can have. Let's take an example to understand this concept better. Imagine you have a piece of wood. The shape of the piece is the mesh object of the 3D model. And the color, wooden pattern, and other visible elements on the shape are the textures of the 3D model. Now if you drop that wooden piece in the water, then it will look a little different than the original wooden piece. Note that it is still the same mesh with the same textures, but it will look different when it is dropped in the water. That difference in the visibility is defined by the shader in Unity3D. The water is the shader in this example. We will discuss about how these are made and applied in Unity3D later in this book.

Materials

In simple terms, materials define how a surface should be rendered in computer graphics. It is not just a container of textures and shaders. Rather it comes with many different properties which vary on the shader itself and gets the reference of the textures to further define the final visibility of the model itself. The following figure shows the difference in two materials with different shaders:

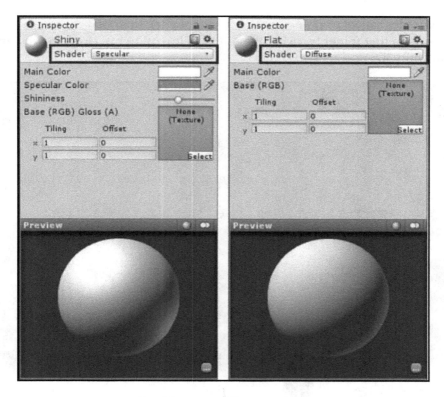

Figure 3.15 Materials with different shaders in Unity

Note the little shine in the left-side material. The reason for this is the specular shader and the right-side material is using the diffuse shader. Both have common properties such as color, base texture, and so on. Unity comes with a lot of built-in shaders, and you can also write your own custom shaders to further polish and define the look of the model.

Applying textures on a farmhouse model

So far, we have given an overview of textures, shaders, and materials, and how they are all connected with each other. But, don't forget that we have an imported model of the farmhouse in our scene which appears in the shade of a white and gray color. Now, we have to apply texture on it and create a material for the model. Unity provides a very easy and convenient way of applying textures on the models.

Create a new folder called Textures in the Assets folder, and load the image shown in the following figure in that folder by using the normal file explorer or dragging the image into the folder in Unity3D:

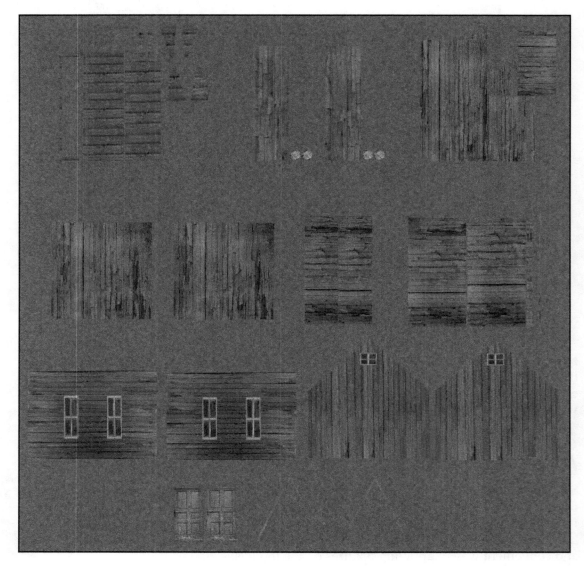

Figure 3.16 Farmhouse model texture

Once it is imported in the `Assets` folder, you have to apply it on the model placed in the Scene view. Drag the texture from the `Assets` folder and drop it on the model in the Scene view and Unity will automatically create a material and do the rendering stuff for you. You can then further customize it according to your requirements. The following figure shows the process of applying textures on the material:

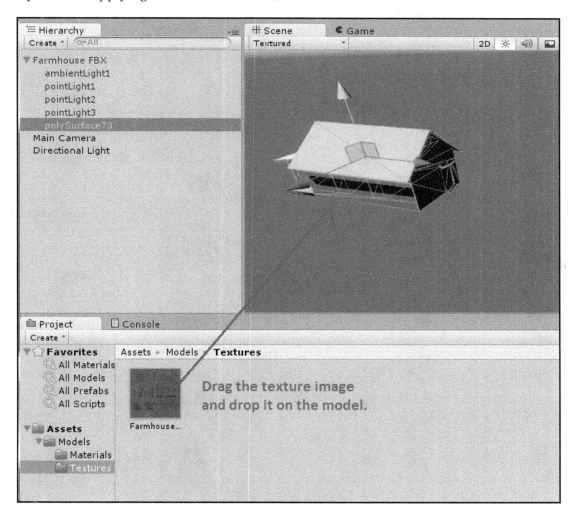

Figure 3.17 Farmhouse model texture

After applying the texture, you will observe that the farmhouse will be in the color form and will look much more realistic now. The following figure shows the simple comparison between before texture and after texture of the farmhouse model and its properties in the **Inspector** panel:

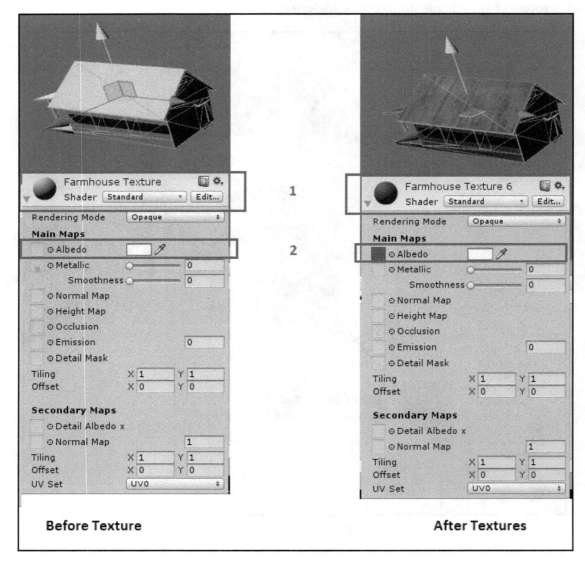

Figure 3.18 Comparison between before texture and after texture

Note that before texture, Unity3D has applied a default texture of the farmhouse texture with the standard shader on the model, which makes it look like a white color. While after texture is applied, Unity puts a numbered name of the texture (called **Farmhouse Texture 6** in the image). Refer to the label number 1 in the preceding figure for the shader. You can also note that the Albedo property (labelled as number 2 in the figure) was empty before but now it is filled with our texture image. You can also apply texture by clicking on the little square shape on the side of Albedo. It will open a popup of the `Assets` explorer panel, through which you can select your required texture from Assets and it will be applied on the model.

Generic and humanoid rigs

Although we have discussed the models and how to import these models in Unity3D, we have not talked about what those models should be or which types of models are preferred by the game engine. A model can include anything from a simple cube with texture to furniture and homes to life characters and aliens to space orbits and planets. In most cases, games are more about the interactive storyline, which involves lots of characters (mostly humans) with many kinds of emotions and expressions. Unity3D, being a very easy to learn and use platform for game development, took this task of providing characters and humans support and offers a highly flexible and fully featured set of tools to handle, animate, and manage character models in a very easy way.

What are humanoid characters?

As it is clear in the word *humanoid* itself, humanoid characters are the characters based on humans. It is not necessary to be a human, but it should be based on the physical shape of humans. The monkey model is a great example of a humanoid model. It could be a two-legged alien and so on. Since most games contain humanoid models, to make things easier, Unity3D provides good feature set for working with humanoid models.

There are a lot of free and paid resources to get humanoid models from the Internet. Or you can create your own humanoid models using tools such as Poser, MakeHuman, or Mixamo. Some of these tools also provide features for rigging and adding skin on the model as well.

Rigging, in simple words, is the process of adding a skeleton and joining bones in any 3D model.

You can also get many free and paid humanoid models of various varieties such as males, females, old characters, warriors, fighters, force characters, and so on, from the Asset Store. Humanoid characters mostly possess bone structure, skin muscles, and textures for costumes or clothing. The bone structure or skeleton, as it is called in real life, is the important thing in any humanoid character. It allows us to repose and animate other humanoid characters with the same skeleton or, as it's called **rigging**. The following figure shows a simple human character with its skin, rigging, and muscles:

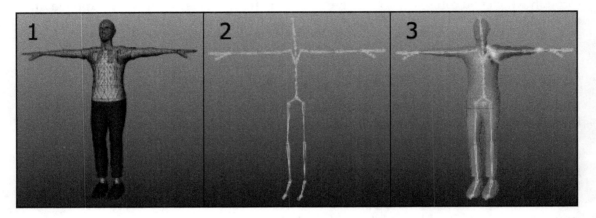

Figure 3.18 A simple humanoid character with skin mesh (left), rigging (middle), and muscles (right)

It should be noted that any humanoid character will have the rigging structure as shown in the previous figure. We will discuss about rigging in the later sections in more detail. Now, we will discuss about what kind of tools are offered by Unity3D for humanoid character models and how they are used. We will learn this by importing a freely available character model from the Unity Asset store.

The Unity Asset store (`http://assetstore.unity3d.com`) is an online marketplace from Unity3D for the assets and ready-made toolkits, add-ons, extensions, and code for usage in Unity games, and is available in free and paid versions.

Importing humanoid models

Let's start learning how to import humanoid models into Unity. We will start from creating an empty project called **Humanoid Character**. As the project is built and compiled successfully, we have an empty project with an empty scene opened as always.

Now, there is nothing different about humanoid models when it comes to modeling formats. A humanoid model is a simple model of file types we discussed in previous sections, such as FBX, MB, 3DS, and so on. We can import those by dragging and dropping the file from the File Explorer into Unity or by manually importing it with the menu option of **Import New Asset...** as well. In this example, we will use a freely available model from the Unity Asset Store. The asset name is Raw Mocap Data for Mecanim and it includes a character developed by Unity3D and a huge collection of animations such as moving forward, backward, jump, crawl, and so on. This can be found at:

`https://www.assetstore.unity3d.com/en/#!/content/5330`. Paste this URL into your browser, and click on the **Open in Unity** button, and it will open Unity3D and show the Asset Store panel with the asset on it, as shown in the following screenshot:

Figure 3.19 Unity Asset Store panel in Unity3D

Now, if you have already downloaded this asset into your local computer, then it will show you the **Import** button; otherwise, it will show you the **Download** button. Download and then import this asset into your Unity project and it will show you a dialog panel with the list of all the files to be imported. This is to let developers know which files are new and which files will get replaced with this asset package. This is shown in the following screenshot:

Figure 3.20 Raw Mocap data files before importing

We have an empty project, so it is showing the **NEW** tab in front of all the files. For now, click on the **All** button on the bottom left section of the panel and then click on the **Import** button. This will take a little time to import, decompress, and import all the assets into the project. Once it is done, you will notice a new directory called **Raw Mocap Data** in your `Assets` folder. This is where all the files and asset data have been placed. This is shown in the following figure:

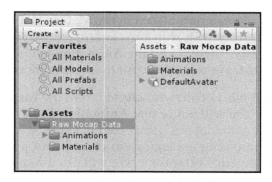

Figure 3.21 Raw Mocap data files into Assets after importing

Since this section is all about the model and its settings, we will ignore the **Animations** directory for now. In the **Raw Mocap Data** directory, you will observe a model called the **DefaultAvatar** file. This is technically an FBX file, if you see it in File Explorer and FBX files are the most preferred model files in Unity3D. When you select it, you will see the **Rig** tab of settings selected in the **Inspector** panel along with some predefined import options as shown in the following figure:

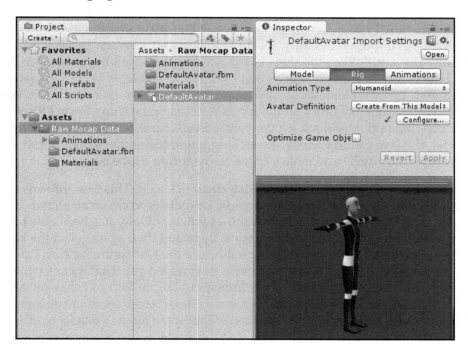

Figure 3.22 Default avatar model import settings in the Inspector

This model comes with many materials placed in the **Materials** directory, which are assigned on the character and show its skin and clothing, as we can see in the small preview section in the preceding figure. There is also the **Animations** directory with a text file containing the animations list. We will talk about those animations in later sections.

So, let's select the **Rig** tab, if it is not already selected from the **Inspector** panel, and discuss the different options there. You will notice that **Animation Type** is already selected as the **Humanoid** option. When any model file is imported in Unity, it automatically tries to detect the type of the model by comparing its rigging structure with a predefined humanoid structure and create an automatic avatar for it. We will discuss this predefined humanoid skeleton structure in the later sections. If it is matched successfully, Unity associates the **Animation Type** to **Humanoid;** otherwise it sets it to **Generic**. There are also two more options, namely **None** and **Legacy**. The **None** option allows Unity to ignore the whole rigging and let the humanoid be without any bones and animations. The **Legacy** option is the older method for handling humanoid characters and it is now deprecated and not recommended to use. You can also manually change the **Animation Type** option of the model. The **Generic** type option is used to tell Unity that a character is not humanoid. For example, it can be some six-legged alien or any horse model, or any strange kind of spider, or any static tree, and so on.

Below the **Animation Type**, you will see the **Avatar Definition** option. Basically, when any humanoid model is imported in Unity, it starts looking for the avatar of the model. An avatar in Unity is a simple skeleton that provides a way to control the mesh, skin, and materials of the model to animate, move, and so on. If the model is already rigged properly and is humanoid, Unity will automatically create an avatar from this model file. We can also copy an avatar from any other model file as well using the **Copy From Other Avatar** option. The copying option will ask for the source avatar, and put the new skeleton in the current model. It is like putting one character's rigging into another's body mesh. It is a very powerful feature of Unity3D and makes character handling a lot easier.

The next option is the **Configure** button with a small tick icon. This icon informs us whether our model is okay to use or not. In simple words, Unity tries to create an avatar automatically from the model and this icon shows whether Unity has been able to do it or not. Select the **None** option from the **Animation Type** and then again select the **Humanoid** option. Now you will see the three dots symbol before the **Configure** button. This tells that the model is not configured yet and the avatar is not created yet. That means Unity hasn't yet acknowledged whether the model file is humanoid or not. You can click on **Apply**, and Unity will try to automatically detect its humanoid characteristics and create an automatic avatar. If the model is humanoid, then the icon will be changed to a tick icon; otherwise, it will be changed into a cross icon, indicating that the model is not properly configured and is not humanoid.

The following figure shows all the different states of configuration of the humanoid model:

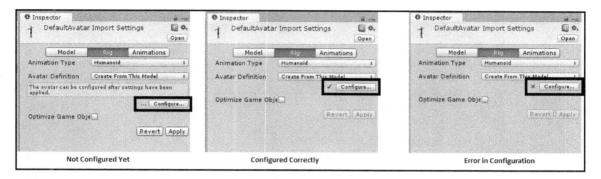

Figure 3.23 Different states of configuration of the humanoid model

We have learned that Unity automatically tries to detect whether the model is humanoid or not and tries to configure it properly by creating an automatic avatar with its pre-defined humanoid rigging. But, we still don't know how Unity does that and what kind of benefits and customizations can be made in the process of Unity to achieve the requirements of our own characters of the game. In the next section, we will discuss about how any character is configured to be a humanoid in Unity and how automatic avatar creation works.

Configuring the avatar of humanoid models

Since the avatar defines the whole rigging and skeleton structure of humanoid models in Unity, it is very important that it is configured properly for the model. We shouldn't depend on the results of automatic avatar creation of Unity. Whether it is configured properly with the tick icon or not configured with a cross icon, you need to go into the **Configure Avatar** mode to personally ensure that the avatar is properly set up and is valid for use in the game. This is a very important requirement for the whole character animation called the **MecAnim System**, which we will discuss in the next section.

Now, as shown in the preceding figure, click on the **Configure...** button. It will ask you to save the current scene if it's not already saved, and will open a new scene as shown in the following screenshot:

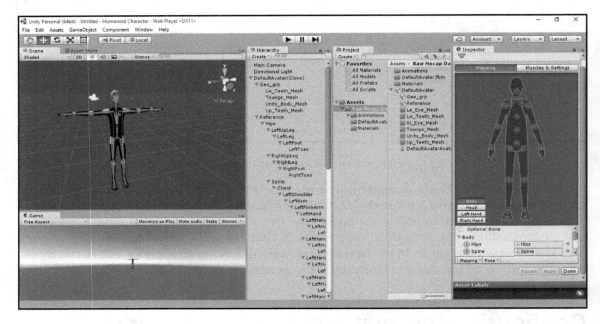

Figure 3.24 Avatar configuration scene

You can observe that a new scene is opened with our character model placed at the center of the Scene View. In the **Inspector** panel, a 2D human character is shown with a lot of green circles within the body of it, as shown in the following figure:

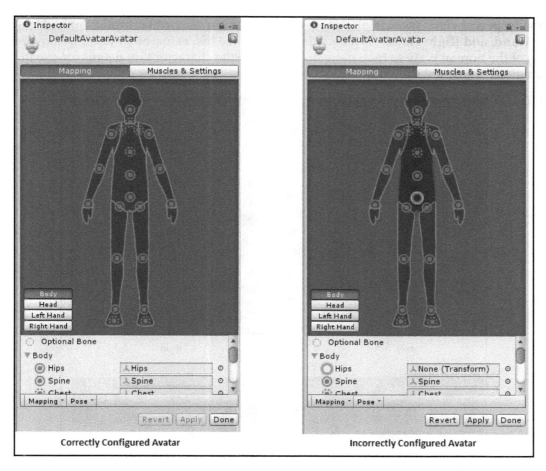

Figure 3.25 View of avatar of humanoid character

This area consists of two tabs, **Mapping** and **Muscles & Settings,** with the first one already selected. In the **Mapping** tab, there is a human body with green circles of solid strokes and dashed strokes placed inside it. These circles map the bones' game objects with the joints of the human body so that it can behave that way. The circles with solid strokes are required to associate with any bone game object. Even if a single required circle is not mapped correctly, then the avatar will not be configured and show a red circle, as shown in Figure 3.25 on the right side.

 To improve your chances of finding a match to an avatar, name your bones in a way that reflects the body parts they represent such as LeftArm, RightForearm, and so on.

In the Inspector view, you can also observe other buttons aligned vertically: **Body**, **Head**, **Left Hand**, and **Right Hand**. As a body is shown in the Inspector, other buttons show other parts of the human body to map more bones to give the character tiny details for use in animations. These are shown in the following figure:

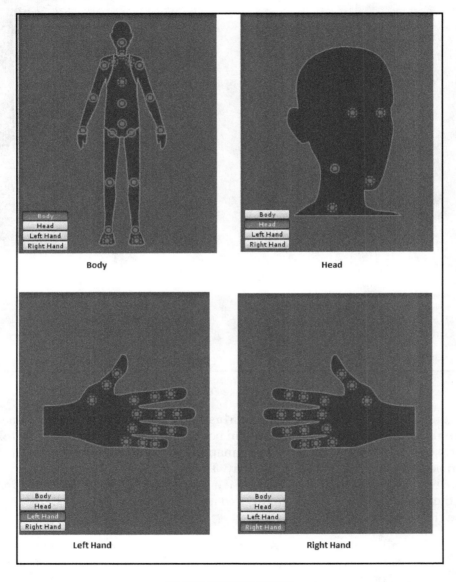

Figure 3.26 Avatar mapping of all parts

You can see that, except the body section, all other sections have only optional bones. And in general, every bone of the human body is covered in Unity. The optional bones are automatically mapped and animated in Unity, but the required bones are to be mapped from the model. And if any one bone is missed while rigging the character, whether it is in Autodesk Maya, or 3D Studio Max, or any other 3D modelling tool, Unity will show a red circle there and it is the developer's job to provide that missing bone by selecting the game object from the **Hierarchy** panel and placing it below the list of bones in **Inspector** panel.

Now, you might also have observed that our character is in the pose of a T shape if you look in the Scene View. If your model is not in the T-Pose, Unity will print the message in the **Scene View** to enforce the model in the T-Pose. The T-Pose is the origin point of the model for Unity to map the right bones with the right game objects. You can manually rotate bones' game objects to form a T-Pose, or you can automatically do it by selecting **Enforce T-Pose** from the **Pose** dropdown in the bottom section of the **Inspector** panel as shown in the following figure:

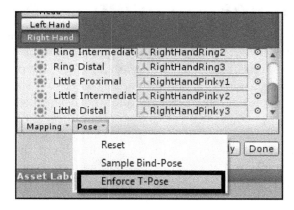

Figure 3.27 Enforce T-Pose option in the Inspector panel

Once the option is selected, the model object will be automatically positioned to the T-Pose if all its bones are correctly rigged and assigned. The other options in this dropdown include **Reset**, which will reset all the bones and sets the avatar configuration to the initial one, and **Sample Bind-Pose**, which will enforce the model to set to the same pose it was at the time of importing the model.

 You can reset the whole mapping and use Unity's automatic avatar configuration by selecting the Automap option from the Mappings dropdown beside the Pose dropdown in the **Inspector** panel.

After any changes you make, you can click on **Apply** or **Revert** to apply or cancel the changes. Once you are ready with the configuration and avatar, you can click on the **Done** button to close the avatar scene and navigate back to your original working scene.

The other tab, **Muscles & Settings,** is beyond the scope of the book, but you can go ahead and experiment a little. It allows you to verify all the bones with the muscles and you can also put restrictions on the movement of bones, such as the head can't rotate fully, by defining ranges in it.

Now, our model is imported and is properly configured to the humanoid avatar. It's time to bring it to life and add some locomotion animations such as walking, running, jumping, and so on. In the section, we will discuss how Unity allows us to manage animations and apply them on the humanoid model objects.

Humanoid animation using Unity

Animations are the core component of any game. Without them, a game is just a sequence of pictures and the user will have no idea of what's going on in the game. We learned about animations in `Chapter 2`, *Finishing the Perky Penguin 2D Game*, for our 2D game, Perky Penguin, to control the animations of a penguin and lasers using state machines and controllers. But, when it comes to 3D, things get a lot more complicated to manage and handle. The reasons for this complexity varies depending on what kind of animations we want to create and manage in Unity, but generally creating character animations such as walk cycle or running cycle takes a lot of effort and cannot be made in Unity. These animations need more details and are developed in advanced tools such as Autodesk Maya, 3D Studio Max, and so on. In this section, we will not discuss how these animations are created, as it is beyond the scope of this book, but we will discuss how these animations are imported in Unity and managed further with programming and state machine controllers to achieve our game requirements of animating a player character for the fighting game.

Unity's animation system allows you to create amazingly animated characters by the support of animation blending, mixing, additive animations, loop animations, time synchronization such as walk cycle, layered animations, animation control playback on factors like speed, time, and so on, and the support of physically-based rag dolls. Unity provides extended graphical user interfaces to make things much easier as compared to previous animation tools such as Adobe Flash.

Legacy Animation System

Before the release of Unity 4.x versions, Unity provided a simpler animation system, now called the **Legacy Animation System**. For backwards compatibility, this system is still available. You can use the legacy system in older projects without updating it to the new system. But, it is not recommended to use the legacy system in any new projects.

We will not go into the details of how the legacy animation system works as it is not a good choice in games in Unity, but we will discuss a basic overview of how it is used in Unity. The Legacy Animation System is based on the following steps to create and manage animations in Unity:

1. You prepare the game object that you want to animate. For example, let's take a fighter character. Now, in order to animate this in Unity, you have to create a model, rig it, texture it, and then import it in Unity. This step is done by artists or 3D modelers and animators.

2. After importing the model, you have to set its **Animation Type** field to **Legacy** manually, as Unity doesn't do it automatically, from the **Rig** tab in the **Inspector** settings of the model. This is shown in the following figure:

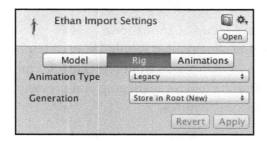

Figure 3.28 Setting Animation Type field to Legacy

3. Now, you set all the animation clips such as walk forward, walk backward, run, jump, and so on, and set the times and speeds of those clips in the **Animations** tab. You can customize and edit clips here with features such as cropping and cutting frames from animation clips, modifying speed, creating loop or Ping-Pong sequences, and so on.

Animation clips can also be embedded in the model file with tools such as Autodesk Maya or 3D Studio Max. Also, animations can be separate files from the model file itself. Unity3D shows embedded animations in the Animations tab of the model file settings here.

4. Once all animation clips are set and ready, it's time to create a controller. The legacy animation system allows you to create a controller in C# or JavaScript, which will tell Unity about which clip to play at what time and for how long, and so on. This controller is basically managed by the game input, for example, on pressing the space key, the character should jump.

Although these four steps don't explain the whole process in detail as to use the legacy animation system, it's enough to get an idea of how the legacy system is used in Unity. The legacy system relies heavily on the scripting part to manage animations and its controller is fully programmed and coded by the developer himself. This makes the legacy system more complex when compared to the new Mecanim animation system, which we will discuss in the next section.

Mecanim animation system

Although Unity had an animation system in place and developers were utilizing it, Unity3D released a whole new system created from scratch for creating and managing more complex animations with a lot more ease. That system became known as the Mecanim animation system. Here are some features of the Mecanim animation system:

-   Easy workflow and set up of animations
-   Supports animation clips created within Unity or imported externally
-   Retargets humanoid animations from one character model to another
-   A visual programming tool for managing and previewing animation clips
-   Layering and masking features

It is possible that you might not have clearly understood some of these features . However, it's nothing to worry about, as we will discuss these features and the system in a lot of detail in this section.

We will start by discussing the Mecanim in our humanoid character project from the previous section.

In the previous section, we imported a free character alongside a lots of animation clips. We discussed the model file and its materials folder, and then we also configured a humanoid avatar for it. Now, we will continue from that humanoid avoid setting and use the Mecanim animation system to animate the character. To do this, first we have to see what kind of animations we have got from the **Raw Mocap Animation Data** asset. Expand the **Animations** folder in the **Project Explorer** panel, then expand the **Walking** folder again to view some of the walk animations.

Now, select any random animation clip from that folder, and in the **Inspector** panel you will see a small preview window with a little **Play** button which will pause/play the animation clip. This whole process is shown in the following figure:

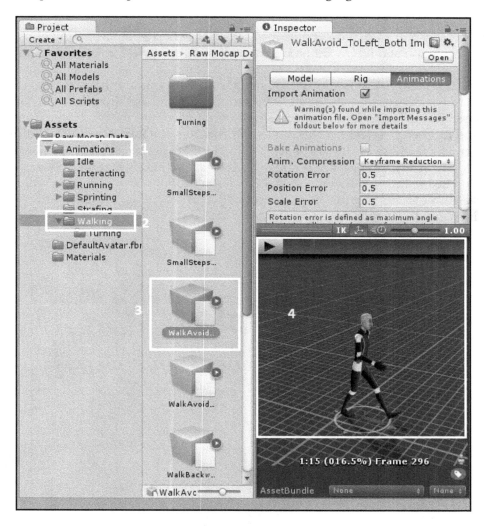

Figure 3.29 Preview any animation clip from the Walking folder

This preview window shows you the animation clip to give you better idea as to which animation is more suitable for your game requirements. You can play more animations from other folders as well.

This preview system of the animations was only available in Mecanim after Unity 4.0 was introduced.

The Unity's Mecanim animation system is based on the concept of **animation clips**, which contain information about how different objects should be moved, rotated, or transformed over time. Each clip can be a different, separate recording of the same object. These animation clips are mostly created by 3D animation artists using third-party tools such as Autodesk Maya, 3D Studio Max, or any other source. Then these clips can be exported using those tools as separate clips or can also be embedded into the model file itself. To understand this better, select the **DefaultAvatar.fbx** from the **Raw Mocap Data** directory in the **Project** panel, and select the **Animations** tab in the **Inspector** panel. You will observe that the **Import Animations** check is already selected, and below that there is an information box telling you that the model file doesn't contain any animation data. That means there is not a single animation clip embedded in the model file itself. This whole process is shown in the following screenshot:

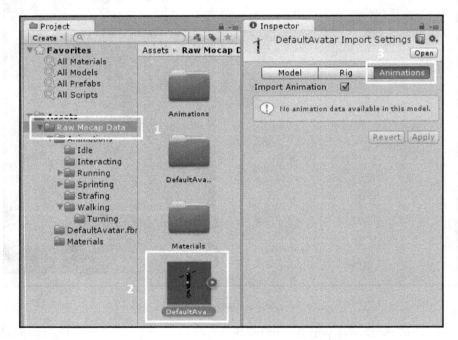

Figure 3.30 Viewing embedded animation data in the model

Whether you get embedded animation clips in the model, or you import animation clips separately (as in this case), these animation clips are then organized into a structure flowchart-like system called the **Animation Controller**. This animation controller plays the role of a state-machine which keeps track of which animation clip should be playing, when the animation clip should stop, and so on. This is one of the most important features of the Mecanim system, which differentiates it from the legacy animation system and provides a lot of ease and control to the developers. In the legacy systems, the developers used to write the whole animation controller using C# or JavaScript programming, but in Mecanim, Unity3D offers a visual interface to create a whole controller without a single line of code with lots of built-in functionality.

Any simple animation controller must contain at least one or two animation clips. These animation clips can be as simple as opening and closing animations of any door or walking forward and backward animations of any humanoid character. A more advanced animation controller can contain dozens of humanoid animations for all the character's main actions such as walking, running, jumping, fighting, and so on. Our game project contains the characters with the abilities to walk, run, jump, fight with hands, legs, and super moves. So, our animation controller for a single character is quite detailed and advanced. In the next section, we will discuss about how an animation controller is created and we will create a simple controller for our player character for the fighting game.

Creating layer character for the fighting game

In the previous section, we discussed the animation systems of Unity; legacy, and Mecanim. In this section, we will not only discuss, but also practically create, the animation controller for our player character of the fighting game. We will use the free character provided by Unity contained in the **Raw Mocap Data** asset project.

First of all, we need a humanoid character in the **Scene** view. Drag the **DefaultAvatar.fbx** prefab from the **Raw Mocap Data** directory in the **Project** panel to the **Hierarchy** panel, and it will show a T-Posed character with a black suit on it as shown in the following screenshot:

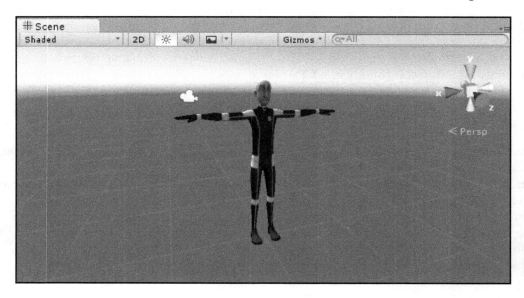

Figure 3.31 The T-Posed character in the Scene View

Now, select the **DefaultAvatar** in the **Hierarchy** panel, and look at its **Inspector** settings. There will be a new component added below the **Transform** component called the **Animator** component, as shown in the following screenshot:

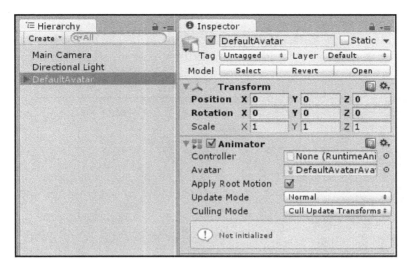

Figure 3.32 Animator component of the character model

You can observe that an information note is given in the component stating that the controller is not initialized. When any humanoid character is placed for the first time in the scene, Unity creates a default runtime animation controller and assigns it to the character. We can also change or modify its controller anytime with our customized controllers as well. There are multiple properties in the Animator component as shown in the preceding figure. Let's discuss some minor details of these properties before moving further ahead:

1. **The Controller** property is used to set the animation controller of the Animator component. This is the most important property, and through this controller the whole character's animations are managed and handled in Unity.

2. **The Avatar** property tells Unity3D about the rigging and avatar configuration to use for the character. This is the same avatar configuration which we set in the previous section of the humanoid character. We can also use some other character's avatar for some other character's animator. That's why Mecanim animation is so powerful and allows developers to retarget their avatar's definitions on other characters without any more efforts.

Now, with the avatar property already set with our configured avatar; let's create our first animation controller. Right-click on the **Assets** folder, and select **Create | AnimationController** and name it **PlayerAnimController,** as shown in the following screenshot:

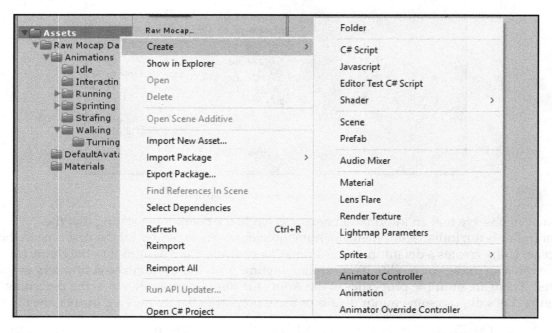

Figure 3.33 Creating an animation controller for the player

You will notice that a different file will be added in the **Project** panel in the **Assets** directory. Double-click on it, and you will be presented with an **Animator** window showing a state-machine-like user interface, as shown in the following screenshot:

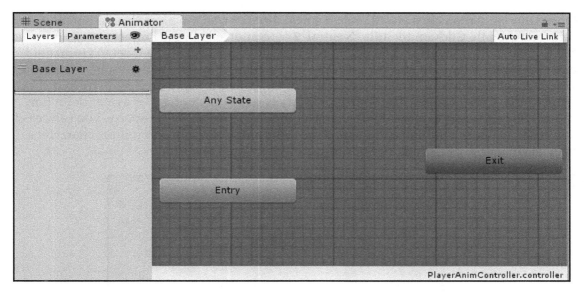

Figure 3.34 The Animator panel in Unity3D

As you can see in this panel, there are three already added states called as **Any State, Entry,** and **Exit** respectively. The primary objective of this panel is to organize all the animation clips, here called **States**, and connect these with each other using sequential, parallel, or more complex relationships using a flowchart-like approach. In order to create a simple state-machine, we need at least one animation state in the **Animator** panel. We already have lots of animations in the project assets imported; we have to just choose a few of those animations for our simple animation controller.

Now, create a new directory in **Assets** with the name of **Player Animations**. I have selected four animation clips from our **Raw Mocap Data** folder and placed those in our new folder:

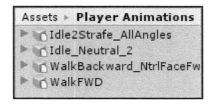

Figure 3.35 Animation states in the Player Animations directory

Once your animation clips are all set in a single directory, let's explore these animations in a little more depth. Click on the **Idle_Neutral_2** animation clip in the **Project** panel, and select the **Rig** tab in the **Inspector**. You will notice that the **Animation Type** is set to **Humanoid** and the **Avatar** definition is set to get copied from another avatar. You must be wondering where the other avatar is. You can select this other avatar in the **Source** property and click **Apply** to save the changes. The Source property is set to our configured avatar definition called **DefaultAvatarAvatar** for our character model. Through this property, you can select any other avatar's definition and retarget the same animation clip on multiple characters very easily. These properties are shown in the following screenshot:

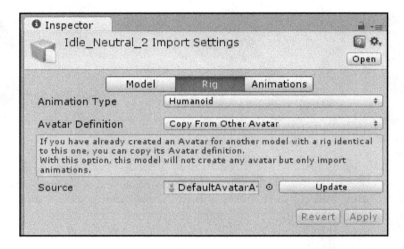

Figure 3.36 Rig tab of an animation clip

The **Rig** tab settings are almost identical for all the animation clips we have got in our project. Now, select the **Animations** tab to customize the animation according to our own project requirements. The partial **Animations** tab is shown in the following screenshot:

Figure 3.37 Partial Animations tab

If you don't want to import any animation, just toggle off the **Import Animation** check and Unity will ignore the animation from that clip. The rest of the settings are not important at this moment and we will discuss them later in the book. For now, the most important setting is the **Clips** property. This is where the whole animation timeline is created. You can observe the **Start** and **End** values for the frames of the animation. You can click on the **plus (+)** sign to add a new sub-animation by defining the start and end frames and Unity will crop that part of the animation in a separate clip. You can experiment with this panel on your own and see what happens on what properties. Also, you can observe a small preview window which allows you to play and stop the customized animation.

Currently, we have only one clip in the **Clips** list and that is selected by default. Below the **Clips** property, Unity is showing you more details of this particular clip, as shown in the following screenshot:

Figure 3.38 More properties of any selected sub-animation clip

You can observe a lot of options here. We won't discuss all of these in much detail, but we will get an overview of this panel here. There are various sections such as **Loop Time**, **Root Transform Rotation** , and so on. These sections define that specific part of the animation. For example, **Loop Time** defines whether the animation as a whole is a loop animation or not. Before every section, there is a color circle with red, yellow, or green fill. This circle tells us about the loop match state of the animation. Red means it's not a loop, yellow means it's somewhat a loop but is not perfectly synced, and green means that it is a perfect loop. These properties allow developers to define the animations in a very detailed way to manage the Y axis position of the character when animating and so on. You can alter the **Start** and **End** values to see where exactly the animation is a perfect loop with all of the green circles and customize it accordingly.

Finally, after discussing many details and properties about animation clips, let's move on to create our simple animation controller. Double-click on the **PlayerAnimController** file from **Assets** directory. It will show the **Animator** view with three states as we discussed earlier. Now, follow these steps to create a walk cycle animation state-machine:

1. Drag the **Idle_Neutral_2** animation clip from the **Player Animations** directory to the **Animator** view. You will see a new orange rectangle added with the animation clip name. This rectangle shows this animation clip state. This is shown in the following figure:

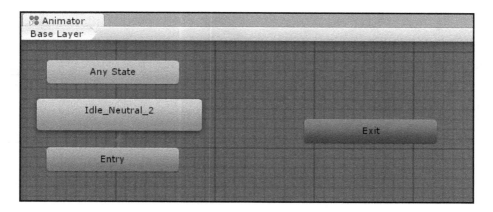

Figure 3.39 New animation added in the Animator view

Any animation can be set as the default animation by right-clicking on it and selecting **Set as Default Layer State** from the menu. Unity will change its color to orange. There can be only one default state in any single layer.

Now, if you play the game, you will see that character in the scene is not animating. Although we have set its default animation state to the idle animation, still the character is not moving. It is because we have only created Animation Controller, but still we have to link the controller with our character:

- To link our character with the newly created animation controller, select the character from the **Hierarchy** panel. Now, drag our **PlayerAnimController** from **Assets** to the **Controller** property of the **Animator** component in the **Inspector,** as shown in the following figure:

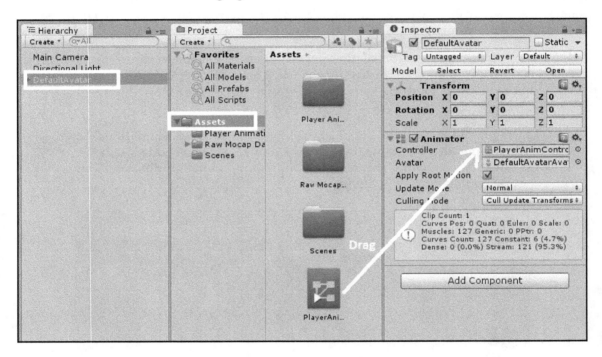

Figure 3.40 Linking character with animation controller

Now, play the game and you will see that character is following the idle animation. But, once the animation is finished, it will stop there. We want to loop the animation infinitely in our case.

- To set the animation loop, select the **Idle_Neutral_2** from the **Player Animations** directory, and go to the **Animations** tab in the **Inspector** settings. Below **Clips**, we have to first set the animation as a perfect loop and make all the circles green. So, set the value of **Start** to 265, and it will turn into green. Also, toggle the **Loop Time** check to on and click **Apply**. Now, play the game and your character will be continuously repeating the animation once it ends. Also, you won't be able to observe the end of the animation, because a perfect loop is created in the animation. This is shown in the following figure:

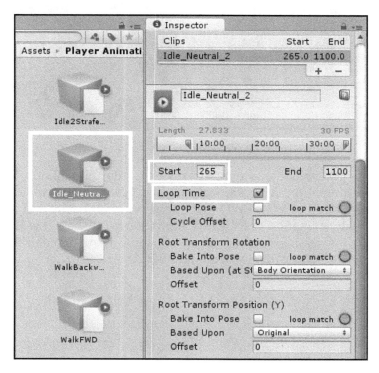

Figure 3.41 Setting animation to loop

- Now let's add another animation state of walk into it. As we did earlier, drag **WalkFWD** from **Assets** to the **Animator** view. It will create another rectangle state, this time with a gray color. This animation state is added in the controller, but it is not linked with the animator. To link this state with our default **Idle** state, right click on the **Idle_Neutral_2** state, and select **Make Transition**. It will allow you to create a white line from the Idle state to another state. Now, click on the **WalkFWD** state and a line will be drawn between Idle and the **WalkFWD** state with an arrow towards the **WalkFWD** state. This is shown in the following figure:

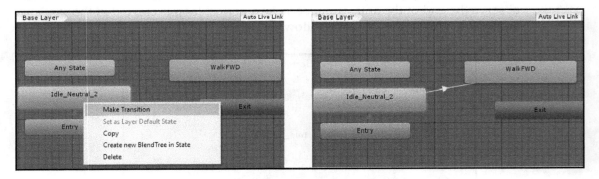

Figure 3.42 Creating transition between two states

Now, play the game and you will observe that once the idle animation is finished, it will start the **WalkFWD** animation. After the walk animation, it will be stopped. We can also create another transition from **WalkFWD** to the **Idle_Nuetral_2** state and this will make the character continuously animate. Once the idle animation is finished, it will start walking, and once the walking is finished it will go back to the idle animation and this will be running continuously resulting in a looped animation.

Now, it's time to add some control in the animator. In the **Animator** panel, on the left side, there are two tabs: **Layers** and **Parameters**. Click on the **Parameters** tab, and click the on **Plus (+)** button to add a new parameter. It will show you a dropdown of which type of parameter we want to add. Select **Bool** from it and name it to **ShouldWalk**. This is shown in the following screenshot:

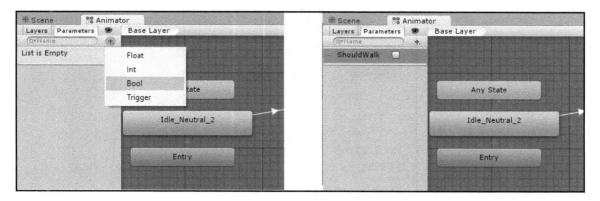

Figure 3.43 Adding a new parameter in Animator

Now, you will see a new parameter is added in the **Parameters** list. The parameters allow developers to control the animation and states flow based on their values. At this moment, the walk animation is automatically started after completion of the idle animation. Now, we will integrate this **ShouldWalk** parameter with the animator so that the walking animation will start if the **ShouldWalk** parameter is true; otherwise, it will go back to the idle state:

To do this, click on the transition arrow of Idle to Walk and check the **Inspector** panel. You will see various settings there. At the end, you will see a small view of **Conditions**. Click on the **Plus(+)** icon from there, and set **ShouldWalk** to true. This is shown in the following figure:

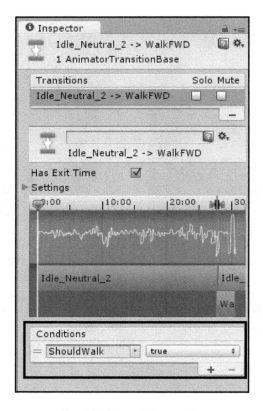

Figure 3.44 Adding a condition on transition

Similarly, now repeat the same process for other reverse transitions as well but this time set the **ShouldWalk** value to false. Now play the game, and you will observe that the character is not going to the walk animation and it is continuously repeating the same idle animation over and over again. It will play the walk animation if the **ShouldWalk** parameter is set to `true`. This can be done from the code very easily.

Summary

This chapter was an introduction to the basic concepts of 3D games. We discussed how any Unity project is configured for 3D games and how 3D model files are imported in Unity. We also discussed the materials and textures for the 3D models. In order to focus on our fighting action game, we discussed humanoid models or character models and how they are imported. We then discussed the configuration of an avatar for the humanoid models to use in the animation system. Unity offers two kinds of animation systems; legacy and Mecanim. We discussed brief details about legacy as it has been deprecated in Unity now followed by a more detailed discussion on the Mecanim animation system. We imported a few animations and worked to create a simple animation controller alongside a simple parameter to control the flow of the animations.

In the next chapter, we will continue from the controller and create a detailed animation controller with lots of animations and parameters, which will be used for both player and enemy characters. We will then control the player movement and animations using virtual joystick controls and discuss a little about artificial intelligence behind enemy characters.

4
Enemy Characters with AI

In the previous chapter, we saw how to import 3D geometry and textures into the project, set up the character and add animation to the character. In this chapter, we will put that knowledge to use and start making a fighting game with basic control scheme.

We will import the player character first and set the different animation frames required for the different animations for the fighting like idle, punch, block, and get hit. We will also be creating the different states using the Animation Controller. Animation Controller let us decide the animation flow based on the behavior of the character.

We will also be looking at game balancing and how to be fair to the player. If the game is unfair, the player will get frustrated and quit the game and will not recommend the game to anyone.

We will be implementing controls using mouse and keyboard but, in a later chapter, we will see how to implement touch controls for handheld devices.

At the end of the chapter we will have a basic fighting system in which we get to hit the enemy and the enemy will take hits or block our attack.

This chapter includes the following topics:

- Importing player model
- Creating player using Animation Controller
- Scripting player controls
- Adding enemy character
- Enemy behavior and AI
- Finalizing the fight

Importing the player model

First, make sure you create a new Unity 3D project. This is not like the first project we created as this is going to be a 3D project, not a 2D project.

Once you've created the project, you will find the `Dude.FBX` file in the assets for this chapter, so drag and drop the file into the Unity project:

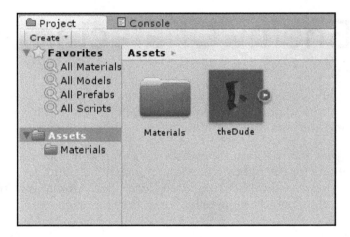

In your case the model will be gray, not red as shown here. To make it red, double-click on the `Materials` folder. You will see the `01- Default` file. When you select it, you'll will get an option to change the color of the object. Click on the gray box next to the **Albedo** option in the **Inspector** panel and select a red color to change the color of the character:

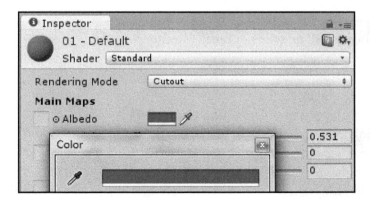

The next thing that needs to be done by us is to create animation clips for all the animations that we have in the game. Click on the **Dude** character in the `Assets` folder of the project. Now look at the **Inspector** pane. In the **Inspector** pane you will see three tabs called **Model**, **Rig**, and **Animations**, as shown in the following screenshot. Click on the **Animations** tab:

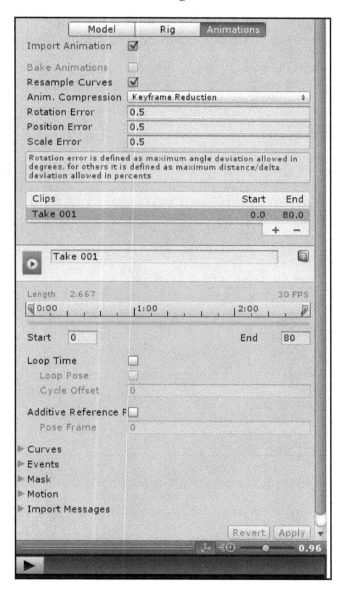

This shows all the animation clips that currently exist. As of now, there is only one animation clip, called Take 001, that starts at 0 and ends at 80 frames. You can even preview the animation by clicking on the play button at the bottom of the panel.

You will see that Take 001 has all the animations that were imported, along with the FBX file, and it has the idle, guard, punch and get hit animations. Since all the animations are in a single clip, we have to break up the animations into individual clips.

To do that, first we extract the **idle** clip which runs from frame 0 to frame 29. So, we change the name to **idle** and set the end frame to 29 for the animation clip as shown in the following screenshot:

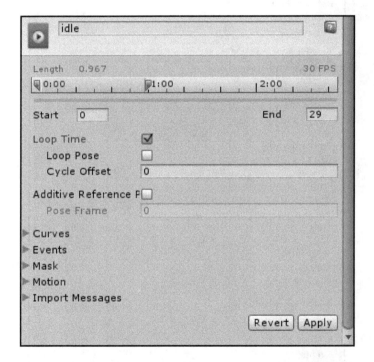

Make sure to click on the **Apply** button at the bottom for the changes to take effect.

Also, observe that the **Loop Time** checkbox is ticked. This is because the animation has to be looped so if we don't check this box, then the animation will just play once and stop.

Now let's extract the second animation clip which is the guard/defend animation. For this click on the + icon in the **Clips** menu. This will create a default animation called Take 001 as shown in the following screenshot:

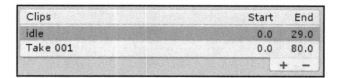

Now, once again, select the **Take 001** clip, rename it to **defend**, and change the start and end time to **32** and **49**. Click **Loop Time** and click on the **Apply** button at the end:

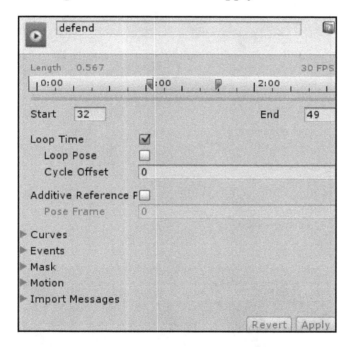

Now add the animation clip for **punch** and **getHit** animations as well. The **punch** animation starts from 51 and ends at 60 and the **getHit** animation starts at 71 and ends at 75.

For these animations, the **Loop Time** option doesn't need to be checked as they don't need to loop. Once you have all the required animations, the **Clips** window should look like the following screenshot:

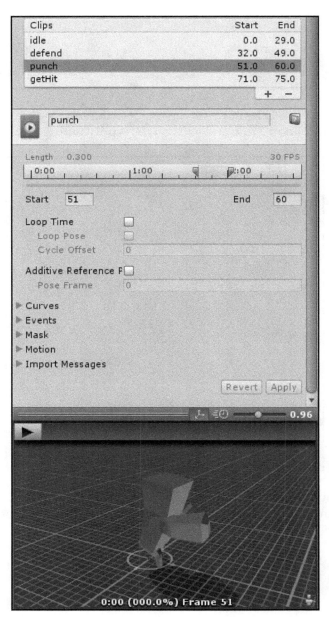

Once we have finished extracting the animations, we can create the Animation Controller for the player character.

Player Animation Controller

To create a new Animation Controller right-click on the `Assets` folder in the project, select the **Create** option, and then select **Animation Controller** from the list:

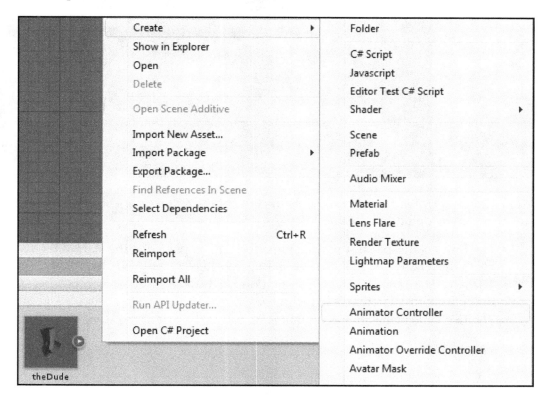

Rename the file to **dudeAC** and double-click on it:

When you double-click on it, a new panel will open up called **Animation**, as shown in the following screenshot:

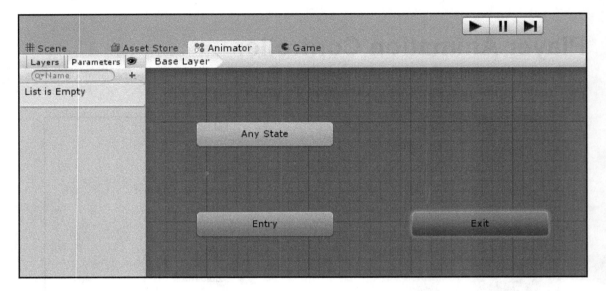

The Animation Controller basically controls the flow of the animation. There are three states that are added in by default; these are **Entry**, **Any State**, and **Exit**:

- The **Entry** state specifies which animation will be played at the start of the scene. So, in most cases the first animation that gets played is the idle animation.
- The **Any State** specifies which animation needs to be executed irrespective of the previous animation that is being played.
- The **Exit** state is the animation that is played at the exit of the scene.

Let's set up the states for the player, which will be the same setup for the enemy as well.

First, we will create the default animation so that, when the scene starts, the idle animation gets played. In the **Animator** panel, right-click anywhere, select **Create** State option from the list, and then select the **Empty** option, as depicted in the following screenshot:

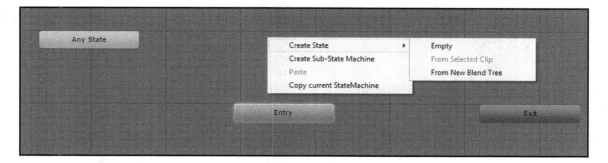

Select the **New State** created and open the **Inspector** panel.

Next, we need to create a transition from the **Entry** state. Right-click on it, a **Make transition** option will open, so click on this option. An arrow will start from the clicked state. Now click on the state that we need to transition. This will create a transition to that new state as depicted in the following screenshot:

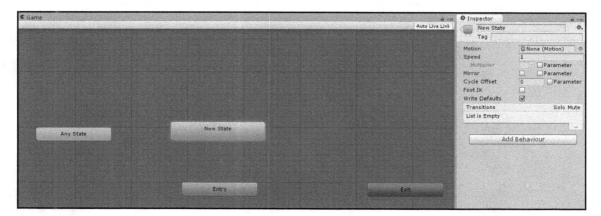

Next, rename the new state to **idle**. Click on the new state and rename the state to **Idle** and change the **Motion** field to **idle** by selecting the small circle next to it:

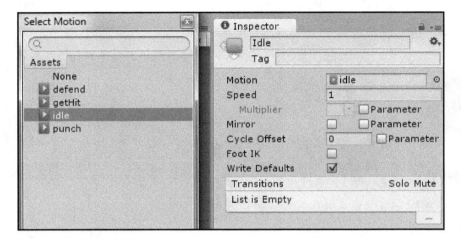

To test if the controller works, drag and drop `theDude` character on to the hierarchy and place him perpendicular to the camera as shown in the following screenshot:

Select the **Dude** character in the scene and in the **Inspector** panel, then drag and drop the Animation Controller on the **Controller** field in the **Animator** component as shown in the following screenshot:

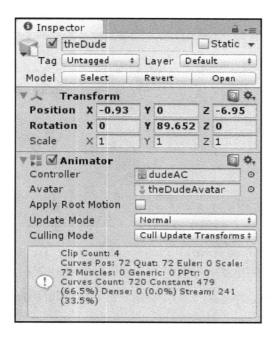

Click the play button up top and you should see the character with the idle animation playing. Now that we are sure that it is working properly, we can go into the Animation Controller and add states that are required for the game.

In **Any State** state, we should be able to have the **defend**, **Punch** and also **GetHit** animations. If the player is not in any of these states then he should revert to **idle** state.

So, in the Animation Controller, add the three states, attach the respective animations in the motion, and change the name of each state accordingly. After creating the three states, we also need to transition between the **Any State** state and each of these states, and when each of the states has finished, it needs to transition back to the idle state.

To create a transition from a given state, right-click on it: a **Make Transition** option will open. Click on it, and an arrow will start from the clicked state. Next, click on the state that we want to transition to. This will create a transition to that state. The transitions are shown in the following figure:

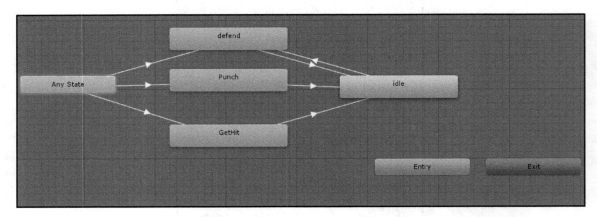

Each of these transitions will be controlled through a script. To trigger each of the states, we will use either Booleans or triggers to enable these state changes.

To create these parameters, click on the **Parameters** tab at the side of the **Animator** panel.

To create a new parameter, click on the + sign next to the search bar. You can either create a float, integer, Boolean, or a trigger parameter.

For our purpose, we created a Boolean parameter, called **bIsDefending**, and two trigger parameters, called **tGotHit** and **tIsPunching**, as shown in the following screenshot:

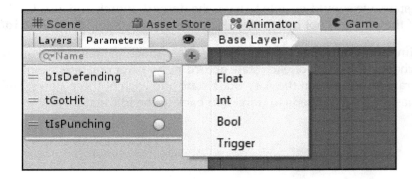

The difference between a Boolean and a trigger is that a trigger will set itself to false once it has been activated where as a Boolean has to have `true` and `false` set programmatically.

Let us see how it is implemented in the current game. First, we'll set the transitions for **Punch** and **GetHit** animations; we will then look at defend after. Select the transition arrow from **Any State** to **Punch**.

You know the transition has been selected when the arrow turns blue. The screenshot shows how the default state looks. We are going to make some changes here:

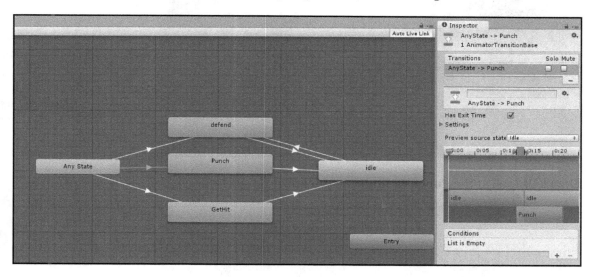

First of all, we want this transition to occur only when the player is punching. So in the **Conditions** tab, press the + sign and add the **tInPunching** condition.

Secondly, uncheck the **Has Exit Time** option. If this is checked then the transition will only occur once the previous animation has completed playing. We don't want that. We want the player to start playing the punching animation as soon as we click the **Punch** button.

Thirdly, and most importantly, the animation preview window shows the animation played during the transition. Initially it shows that the animation will start from zero, play the idle animation, and then transition to the punch animation. We actually only want the punch animation to start immediately, and we just want one frame of transition between idle and punch animations.

So, we bring the **Punch** back to the start and also make the start and stop really small as shown in the following screenshot:

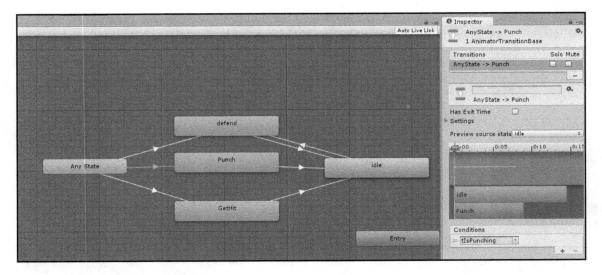

Now let's look at the **Punch** to **Idle** animation:

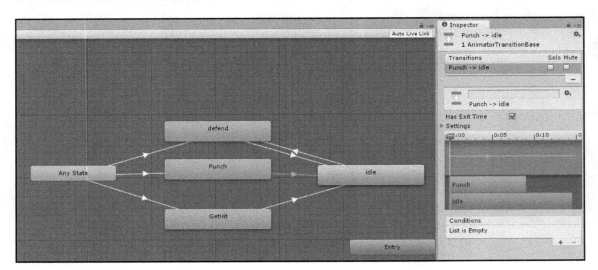

Here, we keep the **Has Exit Time** option checked as we want the animation to finish and then play the idle animation. Also, the idle animation is pulled back to the start and the animation play time is also reduced to one frame.

The same is done for the transition from **Any State** to **GetHit** as shown in the following screenshot. But here the condition is changed to **tGotHit** instead:

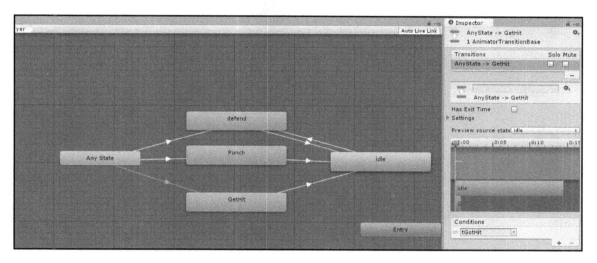

Similarly, from **GetHit** to **idle** state:

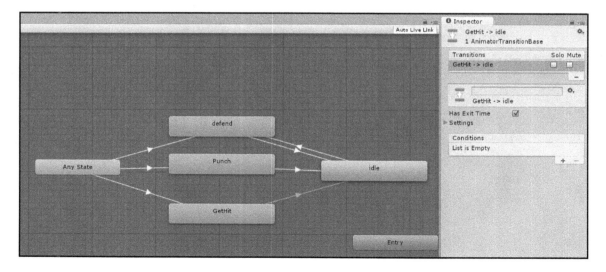

Let's look at how to create transitions from **Any State** to the **defend** state, and then from **defend** to the **idle** state. The transition from **Any State** to the **defend** state should be changed to as shown in the following screenshot:

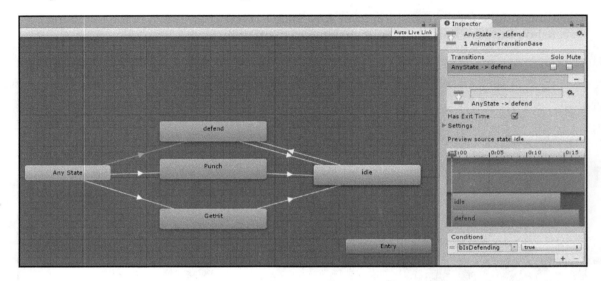

Here, once again, we move the defend animation back and change the play to one frame. The **Has Exit Time** option is checked and now the condition is changed to **bIsDefending**, which is set to **true**. For the transition from **defend** to **idle** animation, we set the **bIsDefending** to **false** and change the animation width as usual:

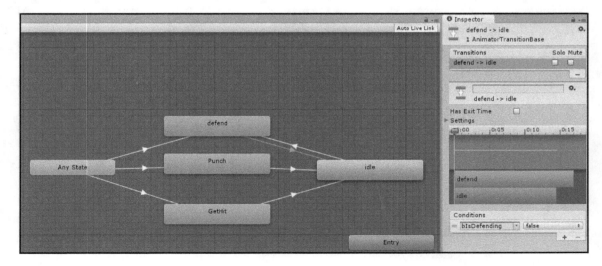

For the transition from **idle** to **defend**, we do it similarly to how we did for **Any State** to **defend**, except we uncheck the **Has Exit Time** checkbox, as shown in the following screenshot:

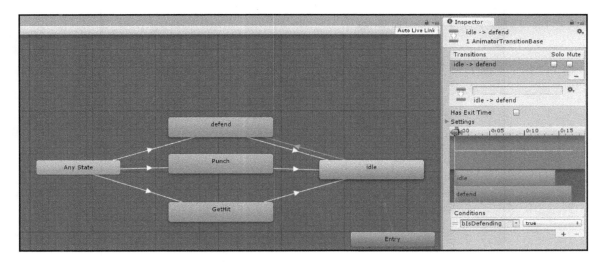

With that we are through the Animation Controllers.

Scripting player controls

To control the states we need to attach a script to the player. We will be using the left and right mouse clicks to control the player. The left mouse click will be for attacking, and the right mouse click will be for defending. If neither are clicked, then the idle animation will be played.

The controls can be changed under Unity's **Projects Settings** option in the **Edit** menu. Select the **Input** option from the list, as shown in the following screenshot:

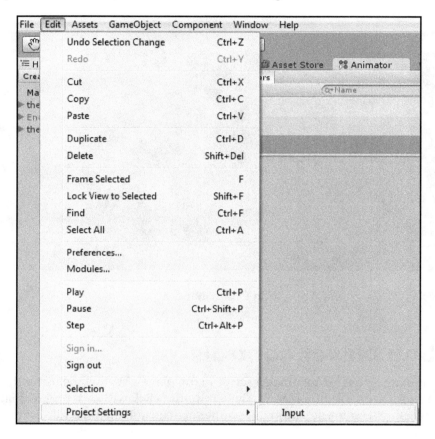

Keep the name in mind, as, while referring in the code, we will be using the name of the button. So, for left-click, we will be referring to the name **Fire1**. You can check the names of the different buttons in the **Inspector** panel:

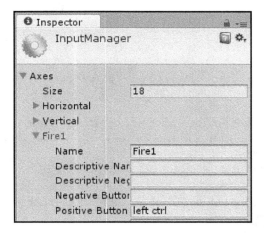

Let's create a new script by right-clicking in the **Assets** folder option ǀ **Create** ǀ **C# Script** and name it `playerScript`. Double-click on it and it should open in Visual Studio.

Add the following code to the script:

```
using UnityEngine;
using System.Collections;

public class playerScript : MonoBehaviour {
    private Animator anim;

    // Use this for initialization
    void Start () {
        anim = GetComponent<Animator>();
    } // start


    // Update is called once per frame
    void Update () {

        //Defending
        if (Input.GetButtonDown("Fire2")){
            // Debug.Log("Jump pressed");
            anim.SetBool("bIsDefending", true);
        } else if (Input.GetButtonUp("Fire2")) {
            anim.SetBool("bIsDefending", false);
        }
```

```
            //Attacking
            if (Input.GetButtonDown("Fire1")){
                anim.SetBool("bIsDefending", false);
                anim.SetTrigger("tIsPunching");
                //Debug.Log("Fire pressed");
            }
        } // update
    }
```

At the top, we create a `private` variable to get the Animator component and store it in the variable.

Next, in the start function, we get the Animator component and assign it to `anim`, as otherwise we would have to do this for every frame which would get very taxing.

In the `Update` function, we first check for defending. If the `Fire 2` button, which is the right-click on the mouse, is pressed then we set the `bIsDefending` to `true`. The `bIsDefending` variable is the same as that we defined as a parameter in the **Animation Controller** option.

If the button is up, then we set the `bIsDefending` variable to `false`.

Next, we set the attacking state. If the `Fire1` button is pressed, then we first set defending to `false`, and then set `tIsPunching` to `true`. We also debug logout so that, we can see the specific code of hit.

To see if this really works, we have to attach it to the player character in the scene and add it as a component: drag the code and add it as a component to `theDude` character. Now, if you look in the Inspector, you can see that the script has been added:

Now, if you right-click on the mouse, the player should block, and if you left-click with the mouse, the player should punch.

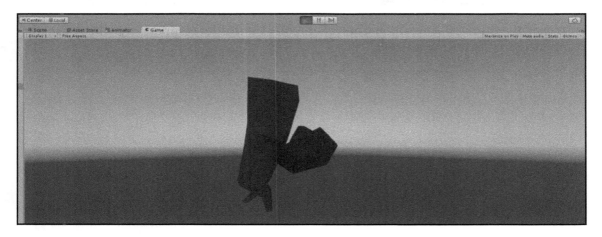

Let's give the player an enemy to punch at.

Adding an enemy character

Just as we dragged the player into the scene, drag theDude character from `Assets` into the `Hierarchy`. Rename this character to **Enemy** in the `Hierarchy`. This dude will also be red, which we don't want, so we'll create a new material.

Right-click on the **Material** folder and then select **Create | Material**. Name the material enemy as `Material`. Change the color next to **Albedo** color control from the default to blue.

Now drag and drop the material to the enemy character. Also place and rotate the character so that it is standing opposite to the player character, as shown in the following screenshot:

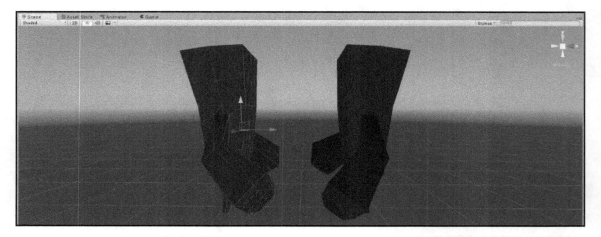

Also drag the dudeAC Animation Controller to the **Controller** component in the **Animator** component for the enemy as well:

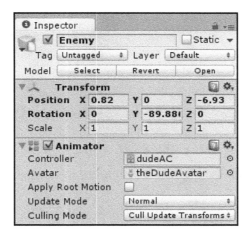

Enemy behavior and AI

The enemy will start with the idle animation as you play the game. Let's add some behavior to the enemy character.

The AI is implemented by creating a pattern, which will determine when the next state change for the enemy will take place, and the period of time that the enemy will either be idle, defend, or attack.

The pattern is an array and has 20 elements in it. After all the elements are exhausted the patterns is randomized and the counter is set to 0 again.

Some intervals last for 10 frames, while others last for up to 120 frames or two seconds. The player has to judge and make sure that he doesn't get hit, and he has to defeat the `enemy` before they kill him. This will make more sense once we go through the code.

Create a new C# script and name it `enemy`. Add the following script to the code.

First, we initialize our variables:

```
using UnityEngine;
using System.Collections;

public class enemy : MonoBehaviour {

private Animator anim;

int myTick = 0;
```

```
int currentTick = 0;
int prevTick = 0;
int nextTick = 0;
int patternLength = 0;
int patterCount = 0;


int[] pattern = new[] {10, 10, 10,30, 60, 10, 40, 60, 120, 30,
                       10, 10,10, 60, 60, 120, 30, 10, 10, 10};
// Use this for initialization
```

In the `Start` function, we get the `Animator` component and set the pattern, which we will randomizing later:

```
void Start () {

anim = GetComponent<Animator>();
anim.SetBool("bIsDefending", true);

Shuffle(pattern);

patternLength = pattern.Length;
nextTick = pattern[0];

} // start
```

In the `Update` function we update the values that we set initially:

```
// Update is called once per frame
void Update () {

    myTick++;
    currentTick = myTick;

    if (currentTick == prevTick + nextTick) {
        int choice = Random.Range(1, 3);

        switch (choice) {

            //will punch
            case 1: anim.SetBool("bIsDefending", false);
                anim.SetTrigger("tIsPunching");
                break;

            //will defend
            case 2: anim.SetBool("bIsDefending", true);
                break;
```

```
        //will be idle
        case 3: anim.SetBool("bIsDefending", false); break;
    }

    prevTick = currentTick;
    nextTick = pattern[patterCount];

    if ((patterCount + 1) >= pattern.Length){
        patterCount = 0;
        Shuffle(pattern);
    }
    else {
        patterCount++;
    }
    }
} // Update
```

The `Shuffle` function randomizes the initial pattern that we created:

```
void Shuffle(int[] a){

    for (inti = a.Length - 1; i> 0; i--){
        int rnd = Random.Range(0, i);
        int temp = a[i];
        a[i] = a[rnd];
        a[rnd] = temp;
    }

    for (inti = 0; i<a.Length; i++){
        Debug.Log(a[i]);
    }
} // shuffle
```

As in the case of the player at the top of the code, we create a `private` variable to store the enemy animator variable.

We also create a bunch of integer variables called `myTick`, `currentTick`, `prevTick`, `nextTick`, `patternLength` and `patternCount`.

The `myTick` variable is just a counter, which keeps incrementing. The `CurrentTick` and `prevTick` variables keep track of the current frame tick and `prevTick` keeps track of the tick when an action last occurred.

The `patternLength` variable keeps track of the number of the items in the pattern array and `patternCount` keeps track of the current pattern number in use.

Pattern is an array containing the intervals for the actions.

In the `Start` function, we get the Animator component and set the `isDenfendingbool` variable to `true` so that the enemy starts off defending. We shuffle the pattern and assign the `patternLength` and `nextTick` to the first element of the pattern.

Next in the `Update` function, we first increment the tick and assign `myTick` to the `currentTick`.

We then check whether it is time for the next action to perform by checking if the `currentTick` is equal to the sum of the previous tick and `nextTick`.

If it is equal, then we create a random number from one to three. Depending upon whether the returned value is 1, 2, or 3, there is a `switch` statement and the enemy will punch, defend, or be idle.

At the end, we assign the `currentTick` to `previousTick`, and `nextTick` to next `patternCount`.

We also need to increment the `patternCount` and to check if the `patternCount` variable's value has exceeded the length. If it is has exceeded it, then we need to reset it.

So, if the value of `patternCount++` is greater than or equal to the value of `patternLegth`, then we reset the pattern to zero and shuffle the pattern, otherwise we just increment the `patterCount`.

Finally, we also have a function which shuffles the pattern so that it doesn't get repeated. Add this script component to the enemy object in the scene and watch him be idle, block, and punch:

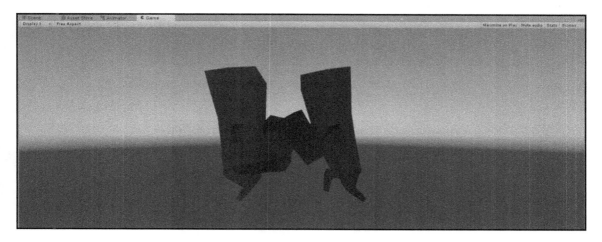

Finalizing the fight

Let us make the player react to the enemy's attacks by changing the behavior of the player. In the `playerScript`, add the following line of code. At the top of the class, create a new `public` variable of type `GameObject` and call it `enemy`:

```
public GameObject enemy;
```

Next, at the start of the `Update` function, get the `Animator` component of the enemy:

```
Animator eAnim = enemy.GetComponent<Animator>();
```

Next, after the attacking function in the update, add the following:

```
// Getting Hit
if (eAnim.GetBool("tIsPunching")){
    if (anim.GetBool("bIsDefending") == false){
        //Debug.Log("I got hit");
        anim.SetTrigger("tGotHit");
    }
}
```

Here, we check if the enemy is punching. If the enemy is punching and the player is not defending, then we set the `gotHit` trigger to be `true`.

Drag `theDude` character to the enemy script component as shown in the following screenshot:

Similarly, in the enemy script add a public GameObject variable called player.

```
public GameObject player;
```

Just before the end of the `Update` function, add the following.

```
Animator pAnim = player.GetComponent<Animator>();

// Getting Hit
if (pAnim.GetBool("tIsPunching")) {
    if (anim.GetBool("bIsDefending") == false) {
        //Debug.Log("I got hit");
        anim.SetTrigger("tGotHit");
    }
}
```

Drag and drop the player in the `GameObject` in the enemy script take a hit when he is not defending:

Now play the game and you will see that the enemy will take a hit when he is not defending:

Also, as of now the player can keep left-clicking and the hero character can keep punching. To limit the number of punches the player can do, add the following code.

Add the following at the top:

```
float totalTime = 0.0f;
float timeSinceLastHit = 0.0f;
float hitTimeInterval = 30.0f * .016f;
```

At the start of the Update function, increment the time:

```
totalTime += Time.deltaTime;
```

The attack code needs to be changed to:

```
// Attacking
if (totalTime>= timeSinceLastHit + hitTimeInterval){
    if (Input.GetButtonDown("Fire1")){
        anim.SetBool("bIsDefending", false);
        anim.SetTrigger("tIsPunching");

        timeSinceLastHit = totalTime;
        //Debug.Log("Fire pressed");
    }
}
```

Summary

In this chapter, we saw how to import an FBX model, import the animations, and set names for the individual animations. We created an Animation Controller and transitions between animations. Once the animations controller had been created, we then controlled the animation using the code.

We also created player controls, created a very basic AI, and controlled the AI behavior with a pattern which we randomized to avoid pattern repetition.

Now that we have a basic skeleton to work with, we will improve this and add a proper game loop in the next chapter.

5
Gameplay, UI, and Effects

In the previous chapter, we created basic gameplay and made sure the correct animation was triggered and the controls are in place. In this chapter, we will finish up the game play by adding a proper game loop so that there is a start, scoring, and gameover.

For the scoring, we will initially use debug to log out the health of the player and the AI. Later, we will look at Unity's **Graphical User Interface** (**GUI**) system and add a health indicator for both the player and the enemy.

Finally, we will also look at the Unity's particle system and the different parameters that we can manipulate to get the desired particle effect for the game.

This chapter includes the following topics:

- Finishing up the gameplay
- Understanding Unity GUI
- Adding GUI for health and gameover condition
- Introduction to Particle Effects
- Creating confetti Particle Effect

Finishing up gameplay

To track the player and enemy's health, we need variables to track how much health both have and how much damage both can do to each other.

For this, open up `playerScript` and add variables called `health` and `damage` at the top of the class. Then, set the value of the `health` variable to 100 and that of the `damage` variable to 10. So, the player will start with a health of 100, and when they hit the enemy, they will do a damage of 10 to the enemy:

```
using UnityEngine;
using System.Collections;
public class playerScript : MonoBehaviour {
    public int health = 100;
    public int damage = 20;

    private Animator anim;
    // other code
}
```

Similarly, add the same code as that of `playerScript` class to the `enemyScipt` class as well. Since we want to be fair, we will set the enemy's health to be 100 as well and set the damage that they can do to 10. Make sure you use the `public` access specifier because only then we will be able to access the health variable when we try to access it in other classes:

```
public class enemyScript : MonoBehaviour {

    public int health = 100;
    public int damage = 10;

    private Animator anim;
    // other code
}
```

Now, whenever the player/enemy takes a hit, we have to make sure that the health is reduced by the amount of damage that other player/enemy can inflict on them. So, in the section of the `Update` function, when we check whether the player or the enemy is getting hit, we have to reduce the amount of health by the damage.

In the `enemyScript` class, for checking if the enemy is hit, change the code as shown here:

```
GameObject player = GameObject.Find("theDude");
Animator pAnim = player.GetComponent<Animator>();

playerScript pScript = player.GetComponent<playerScript>();

//Getting Hit

if (pAnim.GetBool("tIsPunching")){
    if (anim.GetBool("bEnemyIsDefending") == false) {
        Debug.Log("enemy got hit");
        anim.SetTrigger("tEnemyGotHit");
        anim.SetBool("bEnemyIsDefending", true);
        health -= pScript.damage;
    }
}
```

We get the access to the player script by getting the `gameobject` player and adding the `GetComponent` component of the player script.

Once we have access to the script, we can get the amount of damage the player can do and reduce the current health of the enemy by the amount of damage. Now, move to `playerScript`, as we have to implement the same in the player script as well when the player gets hit by the enemy:

```
GameObject enemy = GameObject.Find("Enemy");

Animator eAnim = enemy.GetComponent<Animator>();

enemyScript eScript = enemy.GetComponent<enemyScript>();

if (eScript.isPunching == true) {
    if (anim.GetBool("bIsDefending") == false) {
        Debug.Log("player got hit");
        anim.SetTrigger("tGotHit");
        health -= eScript.damage;
    }
}
```

Here, we will get access to the enemy script so that we can get the enemy damage as we did in the enemy script. Once we have access to the `damage` variable, we will reduce the health of the player by the amount of damage that was set in the enemy script. Now, you can run the game and the `Debug.log` script. The `Player Health` and `Enemy Health` entities seem to be getting affected, as shown in the following screenshot:

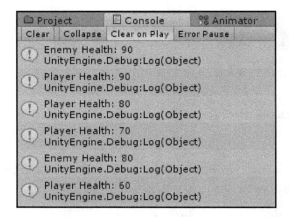

Once we have the player and enemy health being calculated, we can set the game over condition. Once the player's health or enemy's health gets less than or equal to zero, it is game over.

The gameloop is the controller by the third script. We will call this script `gameScript`.

It is a very simple script that gets access to both `playerScript` and `enemyScript`, and it checks for the health of both the player and the enemy. Once either of the player or enemy script becomes less than zero, it announces that the game is over.

So, we will create a new script called `gameScript` and add the following lines of code to the script:

```
using System.Collections;
using System.Collections.Generic;
using UnityEngine;

public class gameScript : MonoBehaviour {

    playerScript pScript;
    enemyScript eScript;
    public bool bGameover = false;

    // Use this for initialization
    void Start () {
```

```
        GameObject player = GameObject.Find("theDude");
        pScript = player.GetComponent<playerScript>();

        GameObject enemy = GameObject.Find("Enemy");
        eScript = enemy.GetComponent<enemyScript>();
    }

    // Update is called once per frame
    void Update () {
        if (!bGameover) {

            int playerHealth = pScript.health;
            int enemyHealth = eScript.health;

            /* Debug.Log("PlayerHealth: " + playerHealth + "
            EnemyHealth: " + enemyHealth); */

            if (playerHealth<= 0 || enemyHealth<= 0) {
                bGameover = true;
                Debug.Log(" +++++ GAMEOVER +++++");
            }
        }
    }
}
```

At the top of the class, we created three variables. The first two are for getting access to the player and enemy scripts. The third variable is a public Boolean that sets whether the game is over or not. Since it is the start of the game and it is not over yet, we set it to false at the start.

In the `Start` function, we found the player and the enemy and got access to the individual scripts using the get component function.

Then, in the `Update` function ,we first checked whether the game is not over. If it is not over, then we get the player's and enemy's health and store it in a local variable called `playerHealth` and `enemyHealth`, respectively.

We then do a check if the player health or the enemy health is less than or equal to 0. If that is the case then we set the `bGameover` Boolean variable to `true` and the `Debug.log` is called, that it is gameover.

Now for the script to actually run it needs to be attached to an object in the scene. It could be a dummy object or any other object in the scene. Luckily we have a camera that is just sitting there and is part of the scene. So, we will attach the `gameScript` to the camera as a component.

Once the script is attached to the camera run the game and see if it reaches gameover condition:

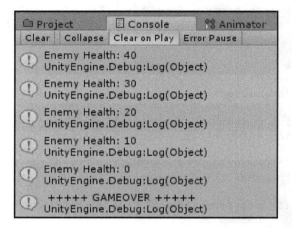

You will notice now that even though the game is over, the enemy keeps punching the player and the player can still punch the enemy. We don't want this as it may lead to some unnecessary bugs in the game.

So, in the player and enemy scripts, we need to get access to the gameScript class and make sure that once it is gameover, nothing updates. In the player's class, we will create a new GameObject called mainCamera at the top of the class as shown in the following code:

```
public class playerScript : MonoBehaviour {

    public int health = 100;
    public int damage = 20;

    float totalTime = 0.0f;
    float timeSinceLastHit = 0.0f;
    float hitTimeInterval = 0.0f;

    private Animator anim;

    public GameObject mainCamera;

    // other code
}
```

In the Update function, we get access to the gameScript complement of the camera and then whatever is in the Update function, we put it in an if condition, which will check whether the game is over.

If the game is not over, then everything inside the if condition will be updated. Otherwise, it will skip through and not update. Here is the updated Update function (no pun intended):

```
void Update () {
    gameScript gScript = mainCamera.GetComponent<gameScript>();

    if (!gScript.bGameover) {
        totalTime += Time.deltaTime;

        //Getting Hit
        GameObject enemy = GameObject.Find("Enemy");
        Animator eAnim = enemy.GetComponent<Animator>();
        enemyScript eScript = enemy.GetComponent<enemyScript>();

        if (eScript.isPunching == true) {
            if (anim.GetBool("bIsDefending") == false) {

                //Debug.Log("player got hit");
                anim.SetTrigger("tGotHit");

                health -= eScript.damage;
                Debug.Log("Player Health: " + health);
            }
        }
        // Defending
        if (Input.GetButtonDown("Fire2")) {
            //Debug.Log("Jump pressed");
            anim.SetBool("bIsDefending", true);
        }
        else if (Input.GetButtonUp("Fire2")) {
            anim.SetBool("bIsDefending", false);
        }

        // Debug.Log("Delta time" + timeChangeInMillis);
        // Attacking
        if (totalTime>= timeSinceLastHit + hitTimeInterval) {
            if (Input.GetButtonDown("Fire1")) {
                anim.SetBool("bIsDefending", false);
                anim.SetTrigger("tIsPunching");

                timeSinceLastHit = totalTime;
                //Debug.Log("Fire pressed");
```

```
                }
            }
        } // check if gameover
    } // update
```

Now, we have to do the similar operations on enemy script as well. Here is the updated code for the enemy class:

```
using UnityEngine;
using System.Collections;

public class enemyScript : MonoBehaviour {

    public int health = 100;
    public int damage = 10;

    private Animator anim;

    public GameObjectmainCamera;

    // public GameObject player;

    int myTick = 0;
    int currentTick = 0;
    int prevTick = 0;
    int nextTick = 10;
    int punchTick = 0;

    public bool isPunching = false;

    int[] pattern = new[] {120, 30, 180, 30, 60, 30, 40, 60, 180,
                           30, 30, 30 ,120, 60, 60, 180, 30, 30,
                           120, 30 };
    int patternCount = 0;
    // Use this for initialization

    void Start () {
        anim = GetComponent<Animator>();
        anim.SetBool("bEnemyIsDefending", true);

        Shuffle(pattern);

        nextTick = pattern[0];
    } //start

    // Update is called once per frame
    void Update () {
```

```
punchTick--;
myTick++;
currentTick = myTick;

gameScript gScript = mainCamera.GetComponent<gameScript>();

if (!gScript.bGameover) {

    GameObject player = GameObject.Find("theDude");
    Animator pAnim = player.GetComponent<Animator>();
    playerScript pScript = player.GetComponent<playerScript>();

    //Getting Hit
    if (pAnim.GetBool("tIsPunching")) {
        if (anim.GetBool("bEnemyIsDefending") == false) {
            // Debug.Log("enemy got hit");
            anim.SetTrigger("tEnemyGotHit");
            anim.SetBool("bEnemyIsDefending", true);

            health -= pScript.damage;

            Debug.Log("Enemy Health: " + health);
        }
    }

    if (currentTick == prevTick + nextTick) {
        int choice = Random.Range(1, 4);
        // Debug.Log("Choice" + choice);
```

Depending on a random number going from one to three, we will choose whether the AI will punch, defend, or be idle:

```
switch (choice)
{
    //will punch
    case 1:
        anim.SetBool("bEnemyIsDefending", false);
        anim.SetTrigger("tEnemyIsPunching");
        anim.SetBool("bEnemyIsDefending", true);
        isPunching = true;
        punchTick = 1;
        break;

    //will defend
    case 2:
        anim.SetBool("bEnemyIsDefending", true);
        break;
```

```
                    //will be idle
                    case 3:
                        anim.SetBool("bEnemyIsDefending", false);
                        break;
                }

                prevTick = currentTick;
                nextTick = pattern[patterCount];//Random.Range(20, 300);

                if ((patterCount + 1) >= pattern.Length) {
                    patterCount = 0;
                    Shuffle(pattern);
                }
                else {
                    patterCount++;
                }
            }

            if (punchTick<= 0) {
                punchTick = 0;
                isPunching = false;
            }
        } // check if gameover
    } // Update
```

The `Shuffle` function rearranges the initial array so that we get a different set of random numbers:

```
    void Shuffle(int[] a) {
        for (int i = a.Length - 1; i > 0; i--){
            int rnd = Random.Range(0, i);
            int temp = a[i];

            a[i] = a[rnd];
            a[rnd] = temp;
        }

        for (int i = 0; i <a.Length; i++){
            // Debug.Log(a[i]);
        }

    } // shuffle
```

Understanding Unity uGUI

With the introduction of the Unity's **uGUI** system, it has been very convenient to set up GUI elements in Unity. We will look at how uGUI works and how to display image and text on to the scene. We will also see how to change the text dynamically in the next topic when we implement the health for the player and the enemy.

All the UI elements in Unity are present in the **GameObject** dropdown in the menu in Unity, as shown in the following screenshot:

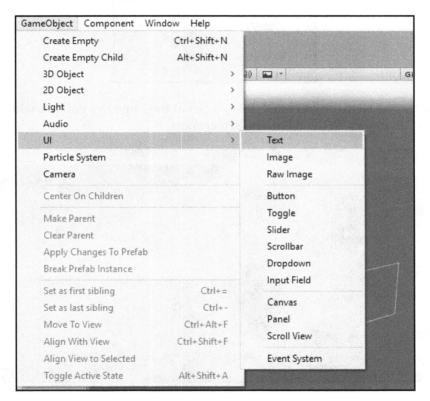

You can create three types of basic UI elements: **Text**, **Image**, and **Raw Image**.

The **Text** option in the menu is a basic text element used to display text-like score, health, energy, and so on. So, like any text element, you can specify text height and font, such as bold or italic. When you create a new text element, there are options such as **Canvas**, **Text**, and **EventSystem** added for each text element that you add:

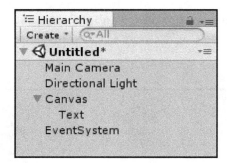

When a new text UI element is created, it is placed at the center by default, with the default text **New Text**, as shown in the following screenshot:

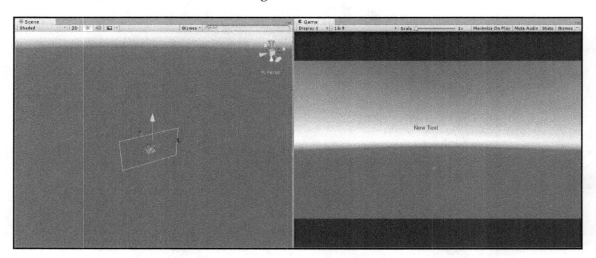

The **Canvas** option in the menu represents where the text component exists in the scene and is also responsible for rendering the text on to the scene. Components to the canvas element can also be added directly by right-clicking on it. You can also add empty game objects to it:

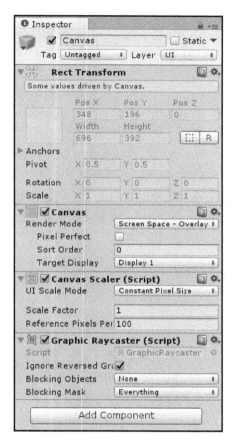

Canvas is made up three scripts: **Canvas**, **Canvas Scalar**, and **Graphics Ray Caster**.

By default, the canvas is set to **Screenspace Overlay**. There is also **Screenspace Camera** and **World Space** options. In **Screenspace Overlay**, the text will set on top of everything in the scene irrespective of whether the camera is in focus. This is used in traditional games where the UI needs to sit on top of the game.

If you want different UIs depending on which camera is selected, you can use **ScreenSpace Camera** and then you can attach different UIs to the cameras. To navigate between the different UIs, you will go back and forth between the cameras for the two UIs.

In **World Space**, the canvas is placed with respect to the world position. So, you can place the button or text in 3D space and position it accordingly. You can move, rotate, and scale the text as well. The user will still be able to navigate and use the UI element. This gives absolute freedom to place the UI element wherever you want in the 3D space.

You can select the **Pixel Perfect** option if you want your text to be aligned to a pixel grid. **Canvas Scalar** will scale the text up and down based on the resolution. By default, it is set to **Constant Pixel Size**. You can also set it to **Scale with Screen Size** or **Constant Physical size**.

The **Graphics RayCaster** script is responsible for getting input from the keyboard, mouse, or touch. If removed, the UI element will no longer accept mouse clicks and keyboard events.

Talking about the **EventSystem** option, let us look at the EventSystem components.

An EventSystem is also created. The event system handles input from mouse, keyboard, and controllers. If you want certain events to be triggers at the click of the mouse, this would be specified here:

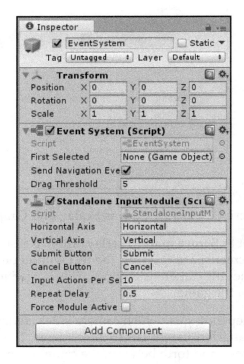

Whenever you create and new UI component and new Canvas and EventSystem is automatically created. Select the text so that we can have a closer look at the component in detail:

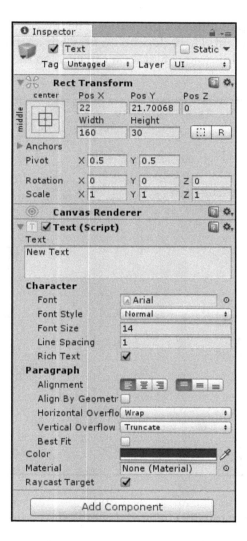

A UI game object is just like any other game object, but unlike others, it has `RectTransform` instead of a regular transform, has a Canvas Renderer, and also has a **Text (Script)** option attached to it.

Rect Transform is made up of different properties. The important one is positions; the others are width and height. These depend on how our anchors are set up. By default, **Rect Transform** is set to middle and center. You can click on the **Anchor Presents** option to change the preset:

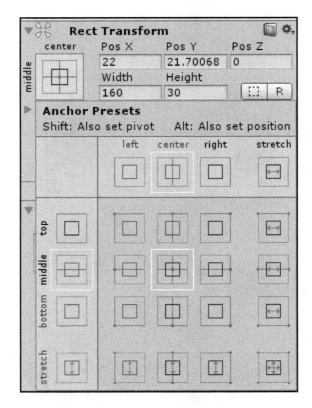

Changing **Anchor Presets** will also affect the **X** and **Y** positions of the button or text on the scene. Anchors can also be manually changed as per your requirement:

Next, we will talk about the **Pivot** field. The pivot is the position around which the UI will rotate. Then, there are **Rotate** and **Scale** fields, which work as other transform objects.

Now, let's look at the Text Script. The Text Script has a text box. This is where you can type whatever text you want be displayed on to the scene.

After that, there is the **Character** section. Here, you can change the property of the character. You can change the font, font style--that is, if you want normal, bold, or italic; size of the font--and line spacing. Note that Unity doesn't let you set the distance between the characters horizontally.

The **Paragraph** section lets you control the position, color, and material of the paragraph itself. You can center align the paragraph, set the horizontal and vertical overflow, or set it to best fit.

Instead of a **Text**, if you add an **Image** UI element, **Canvas** and **EventSystem** are maintained, but the image itself has the usual **Rect Transform** and **Canvas Renderder** properties. Instead of the Text (Script), there is an Image (Script) that is added:

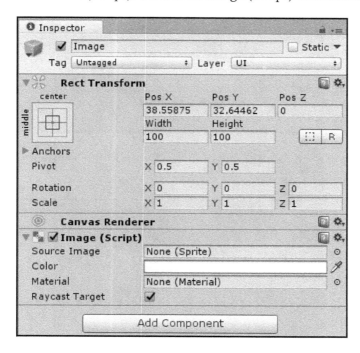

Image (Script) has fewer objects in it. We have the **Source Image** option in which you can specify the image to be displayed. You can change the color or material of the image as well.

With all this information, let's add player and enemy text and also a gameover text overlay, which will appear once the game is over.

Adding GUI for health and gameover

In the game scene, add three texts and name them `enemyHealthText`, `playerHealthText`, and `gameOverText`.

The **enemyHealthText** text is positioned, as shown in the following screenshot, with the anchor at the center and the font height set to 32. The rest are set to default:

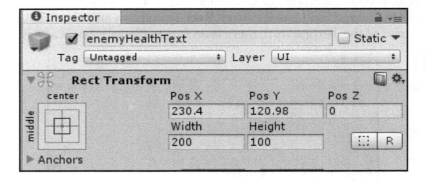

The **playerHealthText** text is set at a position, as shown in the following screenshot, with text height changed to 32:

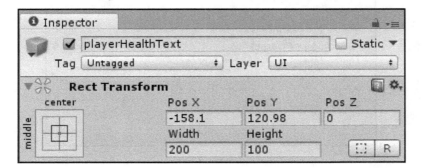

The text color has been changed to blue for the enemy and red for the player. The **gameoverText** text is set to the middle of the canvas, with text height set to 75 and the color set to a nice purple so that it is easily visible.

In the **Text** field, add the text **GAME OVER!!!**, as shown in the following screenshot:.

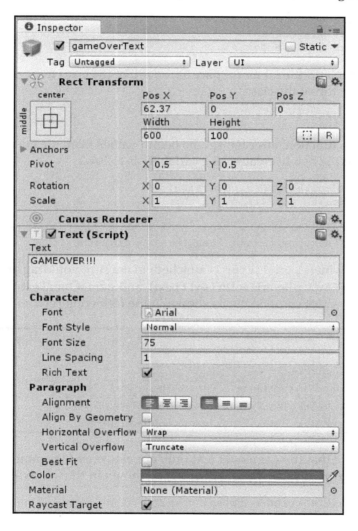

One thing we haven't seen yet is how to control the text by code. Let's see next how to do that.

In the **gameScript** script, add three public variables of type `Text`, as given the following code snippet. This will hold the text object from the `Text` UI elements created:

```
public Text enemyTextInstance;
public Text playerTextInstance;
public Text gameOverText;
```

You will also need to add the UI namespace at the top of the class for it to work, so add the following line at the top of the class:

```
using UnityEngine.UI;
```

Next, in the `Update` function, after we get the health values from the enemy and the player, assign the values to the newly created text variables as follows:

```
int playerHealth = pScript.health;
int enemyHealth = eScript.health;

enemyTextInstance.text = "Health: " + enemyHealth.ToString();
playerTextInstance.text = "Health: " + playerHealth.ToString();
```

In `MainCamera` on which `gameScript` is attached, make sure you drag and drop **enemyHealthText (Text)**, **playerHealthText (Text)**, and **gameOverText (Text)** from the Hierarchy on to the script component, as shown in the following screenshot:

Finally, to make sure that the gameover text only appears once it is game over, in the start function of **gameScript**, disable `gameOverText`, as shown in the following code:

```
gameOverText.enabled = false;
```

In the `Update` function, once the `bGameover` Boolean variable is set to `true`, enable the `gameOverText` as shown in the following code:

```
gameOverText.enabled = true;
```

Now, if you run the game, you will see the score getting updated:

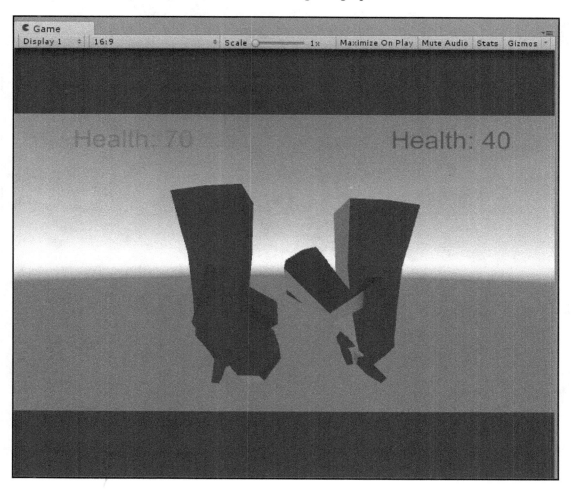

Once the game is over, you will see the gameover text overlay:

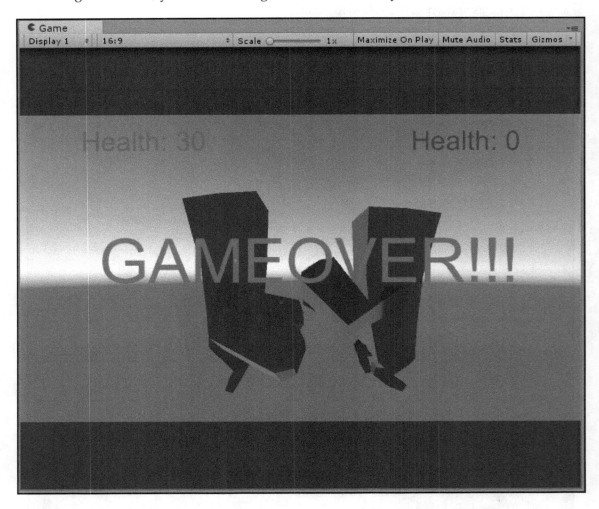

Now that we are done with the gameplay, let's add some effects to the scene using Particle Effect.

Introduction to Particle Effects

Particle Effects are a very big part of a game experience; they add ambience to the game or let us know that something special is going to happen or is happening. We see particles in the form of dust, clouds, rain, and also in the form of the celebration that happens at the end of the game. They can really be whatever you plan to make of them. For the purpose of our game, we are going to add confetti at the gameover.

A particle system in Unity is also a game object, so to create a particle system, go to the **GameObject** menu and select the **Particle System** option:

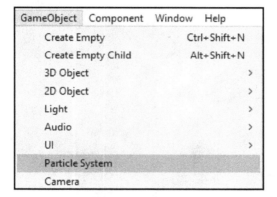

Press the *F* key on the keyboard to highlight the **Particle System** option as it might be created away from the main camera. In my case, it was created at 900, 300, and -26. Don't worry about the positioning of the particle. We will manually change where we want the particle to be created at the end when we want it to be spawned.

Once you zoom in on the Particle System, you will see a cone shape and see particles coming out of the shape. The cone specifies the shape of the emitter, and the white particles are the actual particles that are emitted from the Particle System. This is represented by the following screenshot:

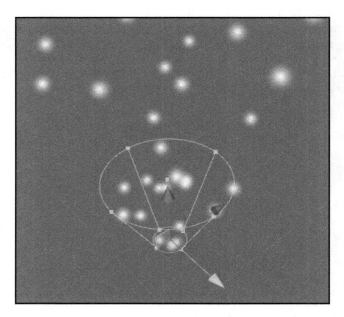

Like any game object, you will also see three arrows that let you position the particle system. You also need to press the *Q, W,* and *E* keys to position, rotate, and scale the size of the emitter, respectively.

Once you select **Particle System** in the Hierarchy, it will show how the particles will be created in the scene. If you select some other object or deselect the Particle System, the animation stops. So, if you would like to preview how the particles are getting created, then select the Particle System in the Hierarchy to get a preview of it.

Let's see some of the important parameters that you can modify in the **Inspector** pane for the Particle System:

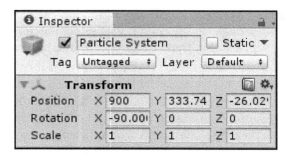

Like all other game objects, you can position, rotate, and scale the Particle System, the first set of parameters are as shown in the following screenshot. These parameters control how the particles are initially created:

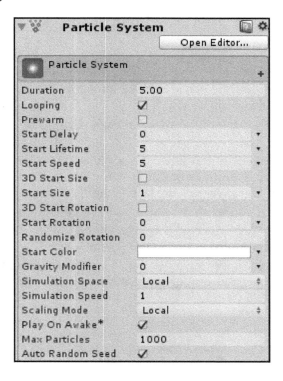

A brief description of all the parameters is given here:

- **Duration**: This specifies for how long initially the particles are created. By default, it is set to 5 seconds. At present, you won't see a difference as looping is enabled. If you disable looping, then if you select **Particle System** in the Hierarchy, you will see that the particles emit for 5 seconds and then stop.
- **Looping**: This should be disabled if you don't want the particles to be spawned continuously. So, if you want a burst of particles, disable looping.
- **Prewarm**: This parameter loads the particles beforehand so that it won't look as if the particles are getting generated at the start of the scene. For example, if you have a water fall particle system and when the scene loads, it should look as if the water fall was running before the scene was loaded. If the waterfall starts to form just after the scene was loaded, it won't look practical.
- **Start Delay**: You can set the particles form after a delay in using this parameter. Right now the particles start forming right after you click the particle system in the hierarchy, but if you want the particles to be formed a second after, then you will type 1.0 and the particles will form a second after you click the Particle System.
- **Start Lifetime**: Each particle lasts for a certain period of time and then it gets deleted from the scene. By default, the particle is always set to be deleted after 5 seconds. If you want the particle to last longer in the scene, this parameter can be changed to cater to your needs.
- **Start Speed**: This is the initial speed of each particle. By default, this is also set to 5.
- **Start Size**: This is the initial size of the particle. By default, it is set to 1. It is the particle object in the initial size that it was created. If you created particles bigger and you would like to reduce the size by half, you will type in 0.5.
- **Start Rotation**: If you want the particles to be generated at an angle in which they were created, then you can set the angle here.
- **Randomize Rotation**: If you want the particles to be created at different angles, then you can specify the angle here. Unlike start rotation, which would create all the particles at the same angle, randomize rotation will create each particle at a different angle.

- **Start Color**: This specifies the initial color in which each of the particles is created. By default, it is set to white. You can change the color by clicking on the white bar and specifying the color.

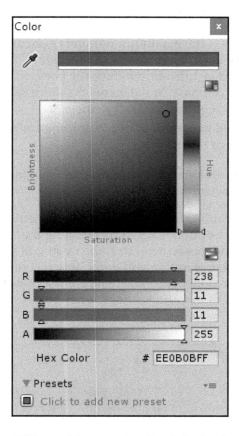

- **Gravity Modifier**: This enables gravity. By default, the value is set to 0, meaning that there is no gravity. If you set the value to 1, you have enabled gravity to the maximum. You can also set the value to between zero and one for an appropriate gravity level as you desire.
- **Simulation Space**: This specifies all the changes that are made after the each particle locally; that is, with respect to the origin of individual particle. By default, set it to local.
- **Simulation Speed**: This specifies the speed at which the simulation is calculated. You can speed up or slow down the simulation. This is useful to see how your particles will behave if you have a particle system that takes time to mature.

- **Scale Mode**: Set this to local. This specifies that the scale affects each particle with respect to the particle's origin and not the origin of the emitter or the world.
- **Play on Awake**: The particles system becomes active as soon as the scene starts. If you don't wish the particle to start immediately at the start of the scene, then you need to uncheck this parameter.
- **Max Particles**: This is the maximum number of particles that can be present in the scene at a time. By default, set it to 1,000. This should be kept as minimum as possible as it would significantly reduce the performance of the game, because the more particles you have in the scene, the more render calls are required and more calculation is required for each particle.
- **Auto Random**: Seed generates a seed to automatically randomize the spawn and movement of each of the particle.

The next set of parameters is optional and requires checking and unchecking if you would like to enable or disable these features:

- **Emission**: This specifies the amount of particles getting generated in a second. The **Rate over Time** option is set to 10, meaning there are 10 particles generated in a span of 1 second. If you set it to 1, then you will see 1 particle each second. The **Rate over Distance** option will work only when World Space Simulation is used. In the **Bursts** mode, you can create a burst of particle depending on the duration that you initially set. So, here, when you click on the + icon, it will create 30 particles every 5 seconds:

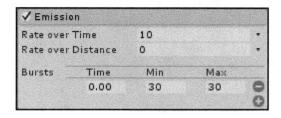

- **Shape**: This specifies the shape of the particle system itself. By default, it is set to **Cone**. Since the Particle System is the shape of the cone, you can see that the particles are generated and move upward in the specified shape. If you want the particle to spread in all directions, then you can specify sphere. You can also select between box, mesh, circle, and edge. By selecting mesh, you can specify a certain mesh and let the particle be generated from that specified mesh shape.

- There are other parameters as well, such as angle, radius.
- **Emit from:** This specifies from where the particles will be generated from, such as Base, Base Shell, Volume, and Volume Shell.
- You can also randomize the direction or align to a specific direction:

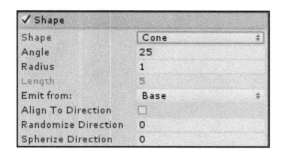

- **Velocity over Lifetime**: If you would like the velocity to be changed over time, then you can specify here. If not specified, then the speed would be kept constant, and it would be the same that was set initially.
- **Limit velocity Over Lifetime**: This can limit the speed of the particle so that once the particle has reached a specific speed over lifetime, it is set either to that speed or slowly reduces over time to the initial speed set.
- **Inherit Velocity**: This controls the speed of the particle depending on the speed of the emitter itself. The faster the emitter moves, the faster the particles are.
- **Force Over Lifetime**: This sets the force of each particle over the lifetime. So, the particle will move faster over a period of time if this value is set.
- **Color Over Lifetime**: The color of each particle can be changed depending on when it was generated.
- **Color by Speed**: The color of each particle is specified by the speed of the particle itself.

Similarly, we have size and rotation, which are either controlled by what stage they are in their lifetime or the speed at which they are moving:

- **External Force**: You can simulate the exertion of external force on the particle by changing the multiplier on the external force, for example, the case of wind.

- **Noise**: You can also generate randomness using noise, which will use perlin noise-like texture to create random movement and behavior of the particles:

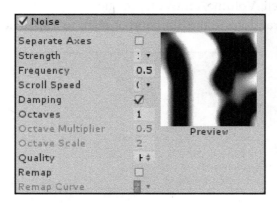

- **Collision**: The particles as of yet won't react to other objects in the scene, so if you place an object in from of the particle, the particle would just go through the object. When you enable collision, the particle will collide with the object instead of going through it:

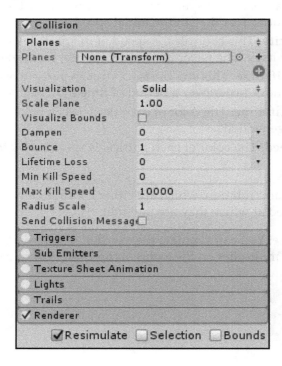

- **Triggers**: Particles can also be used as triggers if the **Triggers** option setting is turned on:

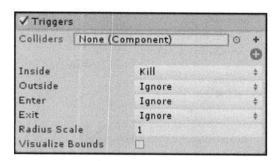

- **Sub Emitter**: Each particle can also emit objects when you enable the **Sub Emitter** option. Also, each particle will also emit other particles.
- **Texture Sheet Animation**: Instead of static images, you can also specify a texture sheet so that each particle is animated instead of displaying a static image:

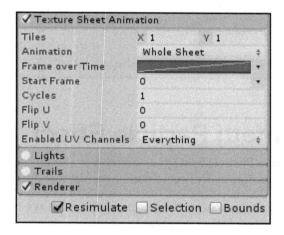

- **Lights and Trils**: Each particle can also have a light source and trails attached to them to make the scene more eye catching and pretty.
- **Renderer**: This specifies a lot of parameters like the shape of the particle itself, if it needs to be a billboard or a mesh. So, in a mesh, you can specify 3D objects such as a box, sphere, cone, and the normal direction of the particle and the material.

You can specify the sort mode, minimum and maximum particle size, alignment, and pivot. Each particle and cast receiving shadows has light probes, reflects light probes, and so on:

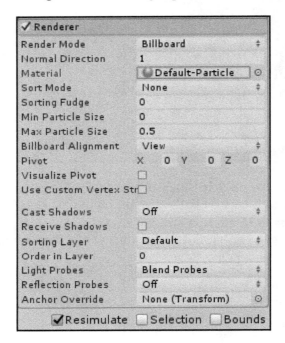

Creating confetti Particle Effect

For the confetti, we create a Particle System as usual. For the initial values, we keep the position to be 0,0,-7.5. For rotation and scale value, we keep at default.

We keep the duration at 4 and uncheck the Looping option as we don't want the confetti to be created over and over. **Start Delay** is set to 0.

Start Speed is set to 5 and **3D Start Size** is set to 0.25 in the X, Y, and Z directions. The **3D Start Rotation** option is disabled. **Start Rotation** and **Randomize Rotation** are set to 0.

Start Color is set to randomize between two colors, red and blue. **Gravity Multipler** is set to 0.125, and we want the confetti to fall down after it has reached its maximum height.

The rest of the initial values are set to default:

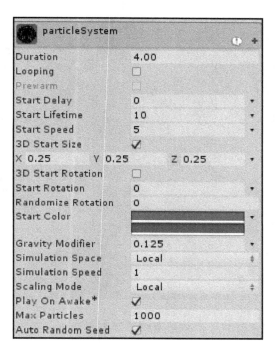

Emission is set to 20 for **Rate over Time**, and **Shape** is set to **Cone**.

To make the confetti more colorful and also change color over time, the color over lifetime is changed. So, change it to your needs. The **Color over Speed** parameter is also changed similarly. Both are set to **Random Between 2 Gradients**.

Size over lifetime is changed so that the size of the particles changes over time. **Size** is set to a curve so that the particle starts out small and then becomes full size at the end of the lifecycle.

The shape of the curve is as shown in the following screenshot:

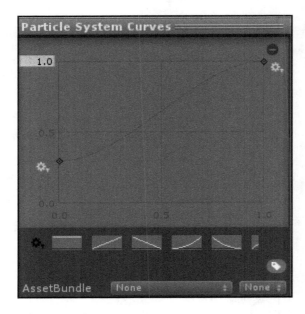

The **Rotation over Lifetime** and **Rotation by Speed** options are set to 45 so that the particles rotate in air once created:

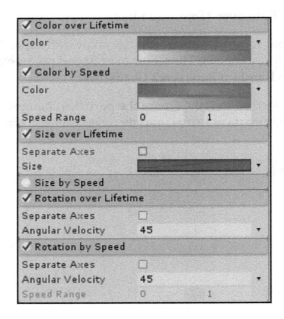

For **Renderer**, I wanted to take 3D objects as particles, so I selected **Mesh**, and for **Mesh**, I selected **Cube**, **Cylinder**, and **Sphere** by clicking the + sign at the bottom. Rest of the values are kept as default:

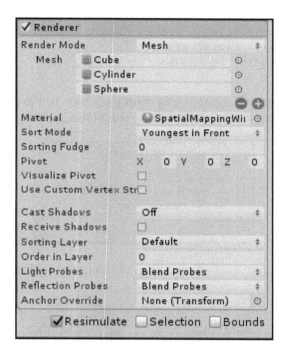

Now, our Particle System is created. We will now create a prefab object in the `Assets` folder and drag the Particle System in it so that we can instantiate the prefab at gameover. Call the prefab **particleSystem**. You will notice that once you drag the Particle System into the prefab, it becomes blue, as shown in the following screenshot. Now, delete the Particle System from the Hierarchy:

Next in **gameScript**, create a new `GameObject` at the top and call it `particlePrefab` and make the variable `public`, as given in the following code:

```
public GameObject particlePrefab;
```

In the `Update` function, after the `gameover` Boolean variable is set to instantiate the particle prefab as following:

```
if (playerHealth<= 0 || enemyHealth<= 0) {
    bGameover = true;
    gameOverText.enabled = true;
    Instantiate(particlePrefab);
    Debug.Log(" +++++ GAMEOVER +++++");
}
```

Don't forget to drag and drop the **particleSystem** prefab on to **Particle Prefab** in the **gameScript** script component that is attached to the MainCamera:

Now, when you run the game and when it is gameover, you will have a nice confetti Particle System:

Summary

In this chapter, we saw how to add in a GUI element to show the player's and enemy's health and also added the gameover text so that we know that it is the end of the game. We also added a very basic particle system just to demonstrate the ability to add particles. You can go in and change the particle system to see what more can be done.

The gameplay is over, and next, we can see how to add in scenes to the game, so we will create a main menu scene, which will show at the start of the game. We will also see how to add buttons so that at the click of the play button, the scene will swap to the gameplay scene.

6
GameScene and SceneFlow

Up to this point, we have only worked with the startScene but in this chapter we will see how to add other scenes to the game, and we'll need a MainMenu scene from where we can go to other scenes, like the options or the achievements scenes.

Each of these scenes will have specific game objects and buttons which will enable us to either change settings or buttons that can take us back to the MainMenu Scene.

The MainMenu scene also needs to have a play button which should link to the startScene which in turn is responsible for starting the game.

Obviously, we can add more scenes and menus according to the needs of the game.

Let us first see how to add buttons to the startScene, so that at the end of the game we can restart the game.

This chapter includes the following topics:

- Introduction to buttons
- Organizing the project folder structure
- Adding a game restart button to the startScene
- Adding a pause button to the startScene
- Adding a MainMenu button to the startScene
- Creating a MainMenu scene
- Adding an Options scene
- Adding an Achievements scene

Adding buttons to the startScene

In the last chapter, we saw how to add text to the scene. However, we can also add buttons to the scene. The button creation process is the same as for creating a text UI. Go to **GameObjects | UI | Button**:

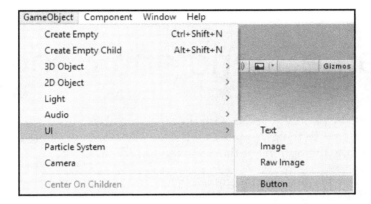

A button will be created in the scene, as shown in the following screenshot:

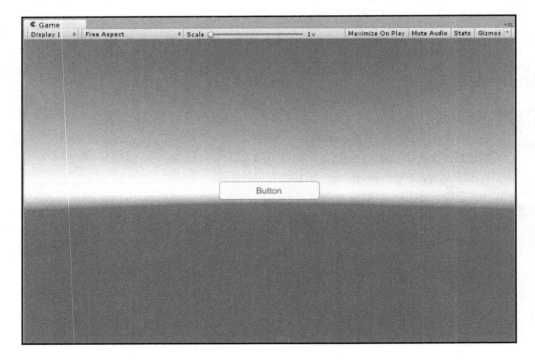

A button will have a Canvas, a Button, and a Text component. If you are creating a button in a scene where a Canvas component already exists, it will just use the current Canvas and create the button beneath it.

We have the Canvas component from the previous chapter. Click on the button in the Hierarchy window.

The button has **Rect Transform**, **Canvas Renderer**, **Image (Script)**, and **Button (Script)** components. We have already come across the **Rect Transform** and **Canvas Renderer**:

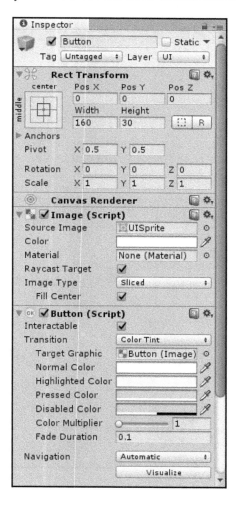

You can specify the image of the button in the **Image (Script)** component. To set the image, you will import an image and convert it to Sprite types. You can only assign it to the source image after you have assigned the image to a Sprite type.

- **Color**: You can specify the button color; otherwise, you can set the default color as white.
- **Material**: If you would like to assign a specific texture it can be done here.
- **Raycast Target**: This allows the target to clickable.
- **Image Type**: You can use the image as it is or you can change it to tiled.

Next in the **Button (Script)** section, we can specify what the button should do once it is clicked. By clicking on **Interactable** option, we specify that the button will change to something else once it is highlighted, pressed, or disabled.

The rate at which the button is changed once it has been clicked on is specified by the Fade Duration parameter.

The **Text (Script)** specifies whether any text need to be shown. If text is appropriate, you can specify the text in the text box. Otherwise you can leave it blank. It is generally better to have buttons that are standard and self-explanatory:

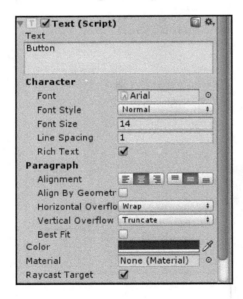

Organizing the folder structure

In the `resources` folder for this chapter, you will see a bunch of images for buttons. Drag and drop the buttons into a folder called `buttons`.

It is also a good time to start organizing your folders a bit. For the sake of convenience and personal sanity, it is better to put assets into folders:

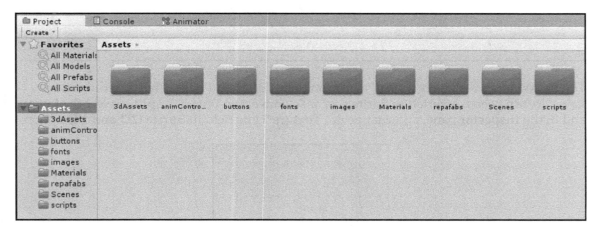

I have created folders structure with the following folders:

- **3dAssets**: Contains player FBX, You can also add other 3D objects, like a 3D environment, and 3D meshes.
- **animController**: I have placed Animation Controllers here. When you have lot of enemies, you will probably have separate Animation Controllers for each, so it is better to also have a separate controller for each.
- **buttons**: Sprites for buttons can go in here.
- **Fonts**: Although Arial is a beautiful font, you might want to choose a font that it is more suitable to your game. So, create a folder to put these here.
- **Materials**: Once again, more objects mean more materials, so get organized!
- **prefabs**: Put all prefabs in a separate folder so that they are easier to access.
- **Scenes**: Scenes are the most accessed files when creating a game, so keep them in a separate folders for easy access.
- **Scripts**: Overtime, you might use a lot of scripts for different things so create separate folders for these as well.

When you open the **buttons** folder, it looks like the following screenshot:

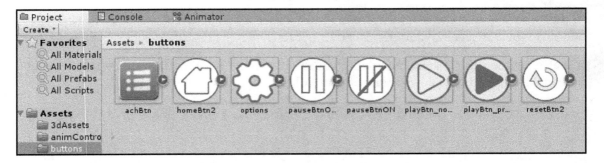

The button images all have a small arrow on their right-hand edge. That is because they have already been converted to Sprite types. To convert an image to sprite, select the image and in the **Inspector** pane, and change the **Texture Type** field to **Sprite (2D and UI)** option:

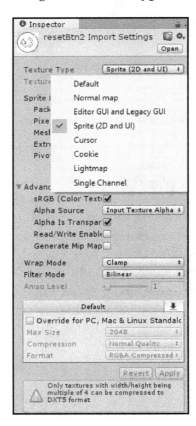

Do the same for all the buttons in the buttons folder.

Adding a game restart button in the startScene

Now create a new button in the startScene and rename the button to **resetBtn** as shown in the following screenshot:

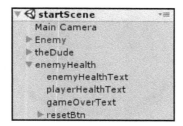

In the **Inspector** pane, under the **Source Image** field, select the **resetBtn2** Sprite type:

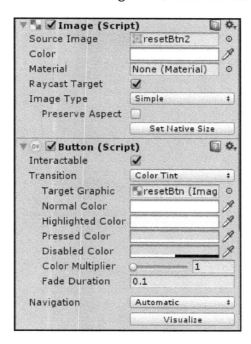

Leave the rest of the parameters as they are. You will also see a preview of the reset button in the **Inspector** pane along with its dimensions:

Position the button so that it is just under and to the right of the **GAMEOVER!!!** text. By this we will make it accessible to the player's thumb:

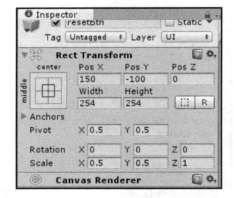

Once positioned, it should look like the following in the game:

Now we have to create a small script so that, when the button is clicked, the **startScene** is called. To do this, create a new script, call it **buttonClick**, and save it in the Scripts folder. Inside the script add the following lines:

```
using System.Collections;
using System.Collections.Generic;
using UnityEngine;
using UnityEngine.SceneManagement;

public class buttonClick : MonoBehaviour {
    public void onButtonClick(string level) {
        SceneManager.LoadScene(level);
    }
}
```

The SceneManager.LoadScene function is responsible for loading the scene in Unity.

When the button is clicked, we will select the `OnButtonClick` function, then pass in a name of the scene to be loaded, and this string will be passed into the `LoadScene` function, which will load the scene itself.

Now create an empty game object by going to **GameObject| CreateEmpty**. Name it **buttonClickGo**. It doesn't matter where this game object is located in the scene. Now add the `buttonClick` script to this game object, as shown in the following screenshot:

Select the `resetBtn` in the Hierarchy. In the **Inspector** pane for the button, you will see an **On Click ()** section below the **Button (Script)** section:

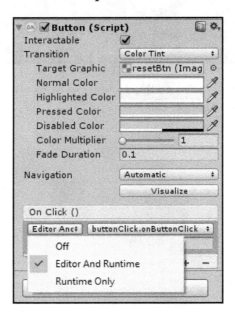

In the first dropdown menu, select **Editor and Runtime** option, so the function can be called inside the editor during runtime.

Next, select the **buttonClickGO** game object from the dropdown list, as shown in the following screenshot:

Then, select the `buttonClick.onButtonClick` function from the dropdown. This is under **ButtonClick | onButtonClick (string)**:

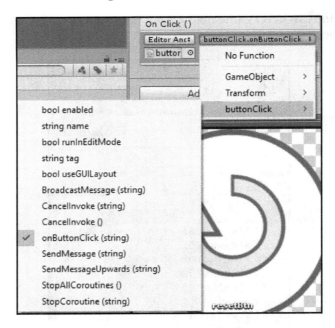

Now, enter the string as the name of the scene that will gets called--in this case we want to call the **startScene**:

We still need to hide the reset button till the game is over. So, in the `gameScript`, create a public `Button` type, and call it `resetButton`, shown as following:

```
public Text enemyTextInstance;
public Text playerTextInstance;
public Text gameOverText;
public Button resetButton;
```

Next, in the `Start` function we set the active property to `false`:

```
void Start () {
    GameObject player = GameObject.Find("theDude");
```

```
pScript = player.GetComponent<playerScript>();

GameObject enemy = GameObject.Find("Enemy");
eScript = enemy.GetComponent<enemyScript>();
gameOverText.enabled = false;

resetButton.gameObject.SetActive(false);
}
```

This will ensure that the reset button won't be visible initially. Finally, once the game is over, update the SetActive function to true again:

```
if (playerHealth <= 0 || enemyHealth <= 0) {
    bGameover = true;
    gameOverText.enabled = true;
    resetButton.gameObject.SetActive(true);

    Instantiate(particlePrefab);
}
```

For Unity to get the scene you want it to load, you need to add it to the **Scenes In Build** list in **Build Settings** option. So, go to **File** | **Build Settings** and click the **Add Open Scenes** button at the bottom, as shown in the following screenshot:

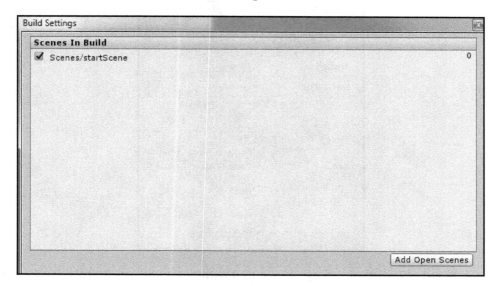

Once the scene has been added, close the window. Now run the game and, once the game is over, you can press the reset button and the game will start again.

Adding a pause button to the startScene

Since we are in startScene, let's add one more type of button, called a *toggle* button, to pause or unpause the game.

Go to **GameObject | UI** and create a new toggle button. Once created, position it at the top right of the game screen. Rename the button to **pauseBtn**.

Like other buttons and UI elements, it has a **Rect Transform** section which can be used to position the button:

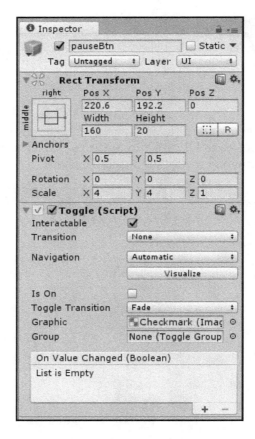

It also has a **Toggle (Script)** which can be set to the default values. Select the **Background** tab, to choose the background image to be used for the button.

In the **Image (Script)** under **Background**, select the **pauseBtnOff** Sprite type as the background image:

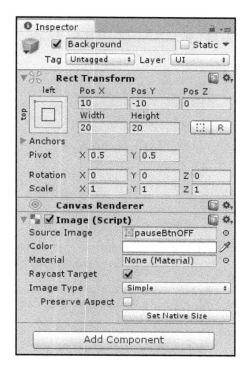

There is also a label tab for any text script, which you can leave blank as we will only be using the image.

Whenever you click the button, it will create a tick mark over the pause image to specify that the button is toggled. If you click on it again it will revert to the usual image.

Now, in the gameScript file, we create a public variable toggle type, called pauseButton, and also create a public Boolean variable, called bIsGamePaused, and initialize it to false. We will use this newly created Boolean variable to go through the player and AI update loop.

So, in the gameScript, add the following code:

```
public Text gameOverText;
public Button resetButton;
public Toggle pauseButton;
public bool bIsGamePaused = false;
```

Next, in the Update function, set the value of bIsGamePaused to pauseButtons.isOn variable. This will set the value to true or false based on whether you clicked on the pause button.

The Update function will look like the following:

```
void Update () {
    if (!bGameover) {
        bIsGamePaused = pauseButton.isOn;

        Debug.Log("isGamePaused: " + bIsGamePaused);

        int playerHealth = pScript.health;
        int enemyHealth = eScript.health;

        // other code
    }
}
```

Next, in the enemyScript, enclose the Update function and check whether the bIsGamePaused is false, in a similar way to how we check if the game is over or not:

```
void Update () {
    gameScript gScript = mainCamera.GetComponent<gameScript>();

    if (gScript.bGameover == false)
    {
        if (gScript.bIsGamePaused == false)
        {
            punchTick--;
            myTick++;
            currentTick = myTick;

            GameObject player = GameObject.Find("theDude");
            Animator pAnim = player.GetComponent<Animator>();
            playerScript pScript = player.GetComponent
<playerScript>();

            // Other game code
        }
    }
}
```

Do the same in playerScript:

```
void Update () {
    gameScript gScript = mainCamera.GetComponent<gameScript>();
```

```
if (gScript.bGameover == false)
{
    if (gScript.bIsGamePaused == false)
    {
        totalTime += Time.deltaTime;

        GameObject enemy = GameObject.Find("Enemy");
        Animator eAnim = enemy.GetComponent<Animator>();
        enemyScript eScript = enemy.GetComponent
                              <enemyScript>();

        // other game code
    }
}
}
```

Now, when you run the game, you can pause the game by tapping on the pause button.

In mainCamera do not forget to assign the toggleBtn to the gameScript script as it is expecting it to be similar to how you attached resetBtn:

Adding a main menu button to the startScene

We will create a main menu button, so that we can press it to go to the MainMenu scene when we select it. To do this, we will create a new button and name it **mainMenuBtn**. Position the **mainMenuBtn** so that it is to the left of the middle of the screen.

Also select the **homeBtn2** option as the **Source Image** in the **Image (Script)** section; and leave the rest of the values set to their defaults:

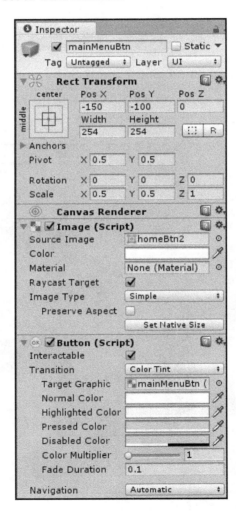

Like the reset button, we can only show the main menu button once the game is over. So, in `gameScript`, create a new public variable called `mainMenuButton`, shown as following:

```
public Button resetButton;
public Button mainMenuButton;
public Toggle pauseButton;
```

Set the active status of the `mainMenuButton` to `false` in the `Start` function:

```
// Use this for initialization
void Start () {

    GameObject player = GameObject.Find("theDude");
    pScript = player.GetComponent<playerScript>();

    GameObject enemy = GameObject.Find("Enemy");
    eScript = enemy.GetComponent<enemyScript>();
    gameOverText.enabled = false;

    resetButton.gameObject.SetActive(false);
    mainMenuButton.gameObject.SetActive(false);
}
```

When the game is over, set the active state to true.

```
if (playerHealth <= 0 || enemyHealth <= 0) {
    bGameover = true;

    gameOverText.enabled = true;
    resetButton.gameObject.SetActive(true);
    mainMenuButton.gameObject.SetActive(true);

    Instantiate(particlePrefab);
    Debug.Log(" +++++ GAMEOVER +++++");
}
```

Next, in the `mainMenu` button object, go to the **Button (Script)** tab and, in the **On Click ()** tab, set it so that it calls **mainMenuScene** when the button is clicked:

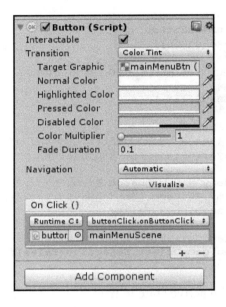

Now, **mainMenuScene** has not been created yet, so we will create a **mainMenuScene** next.

Creating MainMenu scene

Go to the **Scenes** folder in the **Project** tab, right-click and create a new scene:

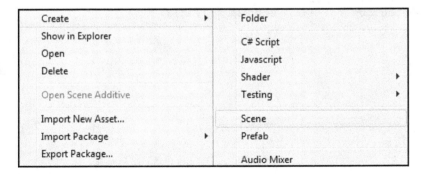

Name the scene **mainMenuScene**. Now you will have two scenes in the project's Scenes folder:

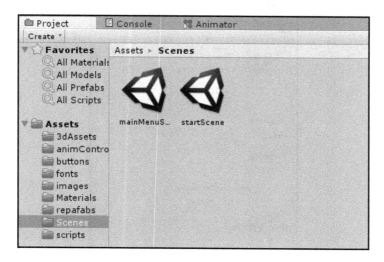

Double-click on the **mainMenuScene** scene and open it. This is a new empty scene, so we will start populating this scene now.

First, we'll add a background image. Go to **GameObject-> UI** and create an Image. It will create a new canvas and an image. Leave the canvas values set to their defaults.

Next, rename the image to `bgImage`. Select the `scenary-ipad` file as the background image, and click on **Set Native Size** option so that the image gets resized.

Next, in the **titleText**, we can add a name for the game, which we will call **PunchyPunch**. In the text box, rename the text to **PunchyPunch**. It is also a good idea to change the font from Ariel. In the `Resources` folder for this chapter, you will find a **duncecapbb** font. Copy and paste the font into the `Assets/fonts` folder. Under the **Character** section, in the **Font** option, select the **duncecapbb_re** as the font.

Finally, change the color so that it is a lighter shade of blue:

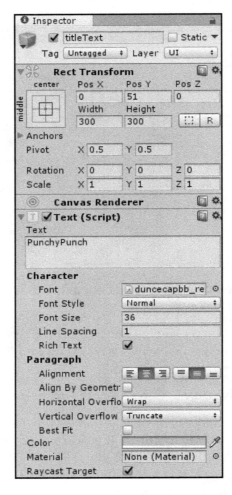

After these additions, the MainMenu scene should be starting to take shape and look like the following:

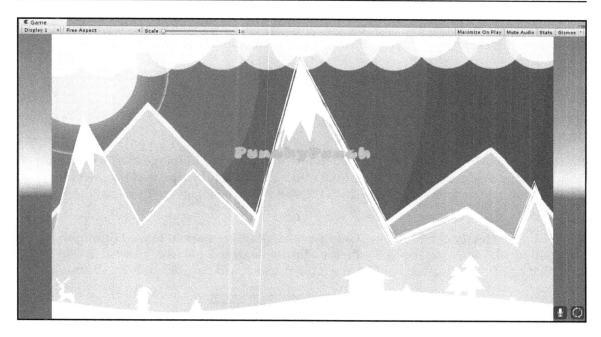

Save this scene.

Next, to make sure **mainMenuScene** gets called when we click on
the **mainMenuBtn** button in startScene, we have to add the scene to the **Build Settings**, so
open up **Build Settings** menu by going into the file and clicking **Add Open Scenes**:

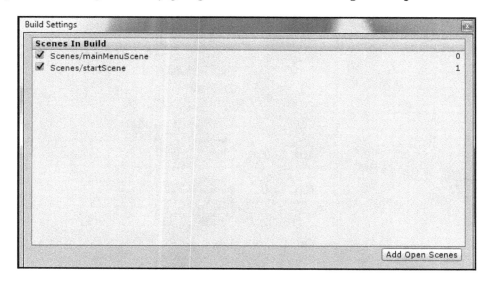

Now, open the startScene and click the play button. Once the game is over the **mainMenuBtn** button will appear. Click on it, and the MainMenu scene should load.

Now let us add a play button to mainScene that will call startScene. So, open up **mainMenuScene** again.

Go to **GameObjects | UI** to create a button. Call this button `playBtn`. It will be created under the current canvas.

Position the play button so that it is at the center of the screen. In **Image (Script)**, for the **Source Image** field, select **playBtn_normal** option. In **Button (Script)** section, select the **Sprite Swap** option **Transition** type field. We will swap the image to show that the button was pressed.

Select **platBtn (Image)** in the **Target Graphic** field; **playBtn_normal** in the **Highlighted Sprite** field; **playBtn_pressed** in the **Pressed Sprite** field; and **playBtn_normal** in the **Disabled Sprite** field (or you could leave it blank as we will never disable this button):

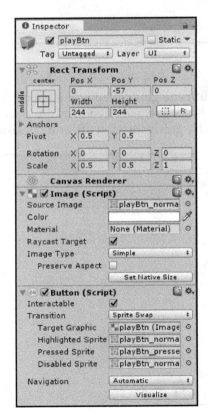

After adding the play button, the main menu scene should look like the following image:

To make the button interactive, we have to create an empty object and attach the `buttonClick` script to it. So, create an empty object, call it `buttonClickGO`, and attach the `buttonClick` script to it.

Now, on the `playBtn` game object in the **On Click ()** section, select the **buttonClickGO**, call the `onButtonClick` function, and pass in the startScene variable to it:

Now, when you click the play button, it will load game by loading startScene.

I have also created one more scene, for *options*. The **Options** scene will contain the functionality to mute or reduce the sound in the game.

To do this, one more button need to be added to the MainMenu scene, as these scenes will only be accessible from the MainMenu scene. Additionally, we will add one more button which will open the achievements window. The button images are provided in the resources folder and you can use these images and place then anywhere in the MainMenu scene as shown in the following screenshot:

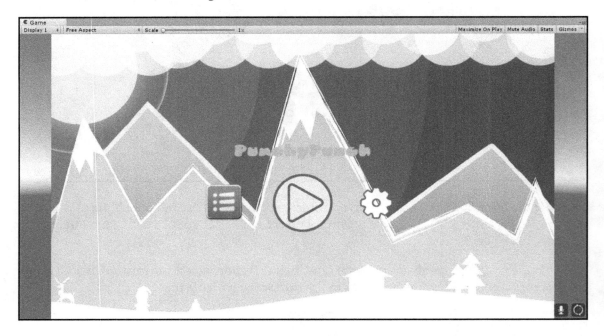

The same buttonClickGO was used so that when either button is clicked, it will take you to their respective scenes.

Obviously, one scene was created, called **optionsScene**. Now the Scenes project folder should look like the following:

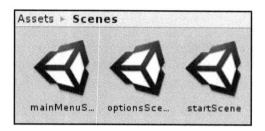

Here is the options scene. There is nothing much here at the moment, but in the next chapter, when we add audio, we will also create a mute button here:

Summary

In this chapter, we saw how to create new scenes and transition between scenes at the click of a button... literally! We added buttons to start the game and travel between the scenes.

We will be using the buttons a lot in the next chapter, when we will see how to add achievements, in app purchases, and add integration. Almost all of these will include the addition of a button. We will also see how to add some different types of buttons.

7

Gamestats, Social, IAP, and Ad Integration

Since we are done with gameplay we can now see how to run the app on a device. We also have an introduction to Unity Ads and In App purchase tools that are already included. We will also include game achievements, and finally, we will see how to upload the APK to the app store and publish the game.

This chapter includes the following topics:

- Running the app on a device/emulator
- Android Developer Console
- Adding achievements to the game
- Saving game stats
- Ad integration
- IAP purchases
- Adding social media integration

Running the app on the device/ emulator

To run an app on a device, you have to get the Android SDK and also the **Java Development Kit (JDK)** and set the location of the **Software Development Kit (SDK)** in Unity.

Let us first download the Android SDK. You can download the SDK from `https://develo per.android.com/studio/index.html`. Go to the bottom of the page and download the command-line tool. You can download Android Studio, but only if you are going to use Android Studio for development, which in this case we are not:

Get just the command line tools

If you do not need Android Studio, you can download the basic Android command line tools below. You can use the included sdkmanager to download other SDK packages.

These tools are included in Android Studio.

Platform	SDK tools package	Size	SHA-256 checksum
Windows	tools_r25.2.3-windows.zip	292 MB (306,745,639 bytes)	23d5686ffe489e5a1af95253b153ce9d6f933e5dbabe14c494631234697a0e08
Mac	tools_r25.2.3-macosx.zip	191 MB (200,496,727 bytes)	593544d4ca7ab162705d0032fb0c0c88e75bd0f42412d09a1e8daa3394681dc6
Linux	tools_r25.2.3-linux.zip	264 MB (277,861,433 bytes)	1b35bcb94e9a686dff6460c8bca903aa0281c6696001067f34ec00093145b560

Download it for your operating system. In my case, I will be showing you how to do it on Windows.

After downloading the folder, create a new folder, in `C:` drive and call it `AndroidSDK` and copy the `Tools` folder into it. In the `Tools` folder, right-click on the `Android.bat` file and run it as an administrator.

You will see an interface as follows. In the packages under `Tools` folder, you will need to download **Android SDK Tools**, **Android SDK Platform-tools**, and **Android SDK Build-tools** by selecting the respective checkbox as shown as following:

⊡ Name	API	Rev.	Status
∨ ☐ ☐ Tools			
☑ 🔧 Android SDK Tools		25.2.5	🗹 Installed
☑ 🔧 Android SDK Platform-tools		25.0.3	📥 Update available: rev. 25.0.4
☑ 🔧 Android SDK Build-tools		25.0.2	🗹 Installed

In the Android SDK version, select the version that is running on your phone. If you have a Google Pixel, you are probably running on Android version 7.1 or 7.0. I have Google Nexus 5 phone and it is running Android version 6.0, so I am required to install it. If you are running on an older version of Android, check which version of the SDK is required for your device:

› ☑ 🖥 Android 7.1.1 (API 25)		
› ☑ 🖥 Android 7.0 (API 24)		
› ☑ 🖥 Android 6.0 (API 23)		

Next, you will also need to install things under the **Extras** folder, which will be required later anyway. You will need to check the **Android Support Repository**, **Google Play Services**, **Google Repository**, and also **Google USB Driver** options from the list to connect your device for installation to start:

∨ ☐ ☐ Extras			
☑ ⊞ Android Support Repository		44	📥 Update available: rev. 45
☐ ⊞ *Android Auto Desktop Head Unit emulator*		*1.1*	☐ *Not installed*
☑ ⊞ Google Play services		39	🗹 Installed
☑ ⊞ Google Repository		44	🗹 Installed
☐ ⊞ *Google Play APK Expansion library*		*1*	☐ *Not installed*
☐ ⊞ *Google Play Licensing Library*		*1*	☐ *Not installed*
☐ ⊞ *Google Play Billing Library*		*5*	☐ *Not installed*
☐ ⊞ *Android Auto API Simulators*		*1*	☐ *Not installed*
☑ ⊞ *Google USB Driver*		*11*	☐ *Not installed*

Select all the options, accept the terms, and click the install button for the installation to start:

While that is getting installed, let's also download the JDK. To download the SDK go to this link `http://www.oracle.com/technetwork/java/javase/downloads/jdk8-downloads-2133151.html` and download the version for your operating system.

Java SE Development Kit 8u121

You must accept the Oracle Binary Code License Agreement for Java SE to download this software.

◯ Accept License Agreement   ◉ Decline License Agreement

Product / File Description	File Size	Download
Linux ARM 32 Hard Float ABI	77.86 MB	⬇ jdk-8u121-linux-arm32-vfp-hflt.tar.gz
Linux ARM 64 Hard Float ABI	74.83 MB	⬇ jdk-8u121-linux-arm64-vfp-hflt.tar.gz
Linux x86	162.41 MB	⬇ jdk-8u121-linux-i586.rpm
Linux x86	177.13 MB	⬇ jdk-8u121-linux-i586.tar.gz
Linux x64	159.96 MB	⬇ jdk-8u121-linux-x64.rpm
Linux x64	174.76 MB	⬇ jdk-8u121-linux-x64.tar.gz
Mac OS X	223.21 MB	⬇ jdk-8u121-macosx-x64.dmg
Solaris SPARC 64-bit	139.64 MB	⬇ jdk-8u121-solaris-sparcv9.tar.Z
Solaris SPARC 64-bit	99.07 MB	⬇ jdk-8u121-solaris-sparcv9.tar.gz
Solaris x64	140.42 MB	⬇ jdk-8u121-solaris-x64.tar.Z
Solaris x64	96.9 MB	⬇ jdk-8u121-solaris-x64.tar.gz
Windows x86	189.36 MB	⬇ jdk-8u121-windows-i586.exe
Windows x64	195.51 MB	⬇ jdk-8u121-windows-x64.exe

There is no need to download demos and samples. Once downloaded, install it at the default location.

You will also need to download the Unity Android module. Go to **File** | **Build Settings** and select the **Android** in the **Platform** section. It will say *No Android Module Loaded*. Click on the **Open Download** page. Once you click the button, the download should start and once downloaded, it should be inside the `Downloads` folder. You can also download it from `http://download.unity3d.com/download_unity/38b4efef76f0/TargetSupportInstaller/UnitySetup-Android-Support-for-Editor-5.5.0f3.exe`. Make sure you change the version number to the one that you are currently running. Once downloaded, open the Unity project and then double-click on the Android module to install the required package.

Now go to **Build Settings** and select the **Android** platform and click on the **Switch Platform** button at the bottom:

Now we have to set the path for the `AndroidSDK` folder and JDK in Unity. Go to **Edit** menu and open **Preferences** under the **External tools** option, then browse to the SDK and JDK locations:

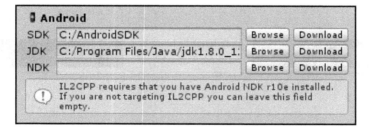

The Android SDK location is at `C:/ AndroidSDK` and for the JDK it is located at `C:/Program Files/Java/jdk1.8.0_121`.

Now we have to prepare the Android device, enable the **Developer Options** mode in the device, and enable USB debugging. On the device, go to **Settings** and **About Phone** and at the bottom you will find the **Build Number**, tap on it seven times. It will then tell you that you are a developer now:

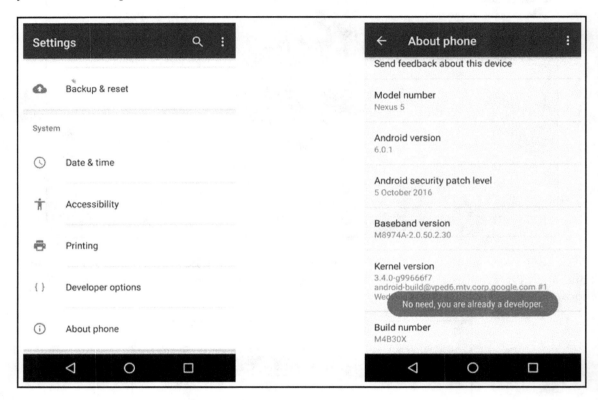

Press back key and go into **Developer Options**. Enable the **USB debugging** and **Stay awake** options:

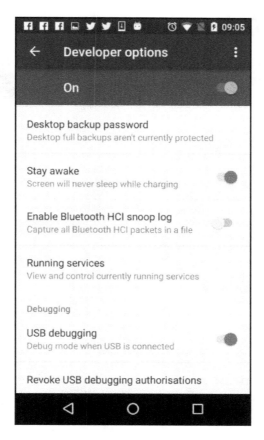

And that should be it. Now your device is ready to build on the device.

Android Developer Console

Now, to test/publish your game or to add achievements, you will need to upload your app to the Android's **Developer Console**. It has a one-time fee of 25 USD. Once paid, you can publish and test as many games/apps as you want.

If you have your Gmail ID ready, head on to `https://play.google.com/apps/publish/si gnup/#;` to sign up as an Android developer. The following window will be displayed:

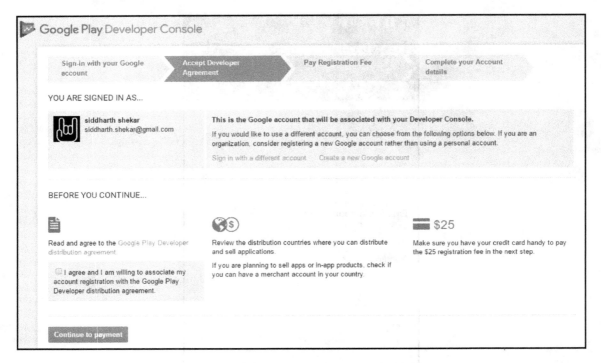

Click on the **Continue to payment** button and have your credit card ready. Once payment is made, you will have access to the Developer Console. Congratulations! You are an Android developer now.

You will be greeted with the following screen. I already have some games and apps on the android store, so your existing apps will show up here:

While we are here, let us create a new app. Click on the **+ Create application** button on the top-right corner:

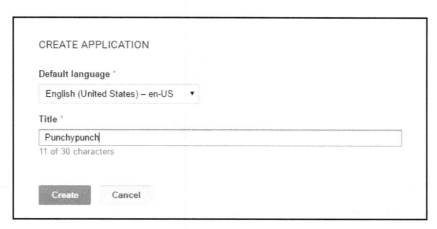

In the dialog box, specify the language and title of the game here. Next specify the details in the **Title** and **Short description** fields and then click on the **Save Draft** button at the top-right corner of the window:

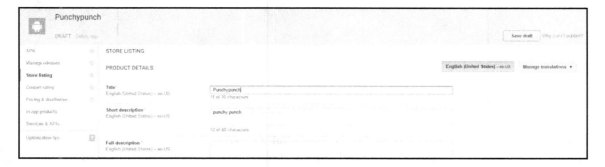

Next click on the **APK** tab on the left, as we will have to upload an APK to add achievements:

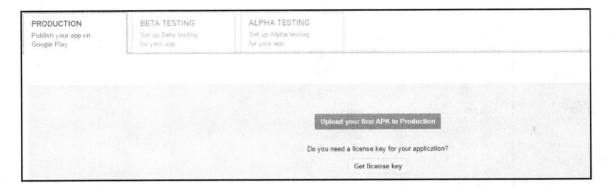

Click on **Upload your first APK to Production**. Now we have to upload the APK to the page:

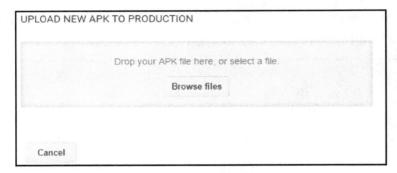

Let's us go back to Unity and build the APK so that we can upload to the Developer Console. In Unity, go to **Edit** | **Build Settings** and click on the **PlayerSettings** option.

Under **PlayerSettings**, type in the details in the **Company Name** and **Product Name** fields. Don't worry about icons now; we will add them later.

Under the **Other Settings** section, add a bundle identifier. This is always the reverse order of your company website followed by the product name. Add the version number, which is 1.0. The bundle version code can be 1. Lastly add the minimum Android API level that the application can support. I have chosen Marshmallow, but the lower the number is, the better, so the application can be enjoyed by people even with older phones running older android versions:

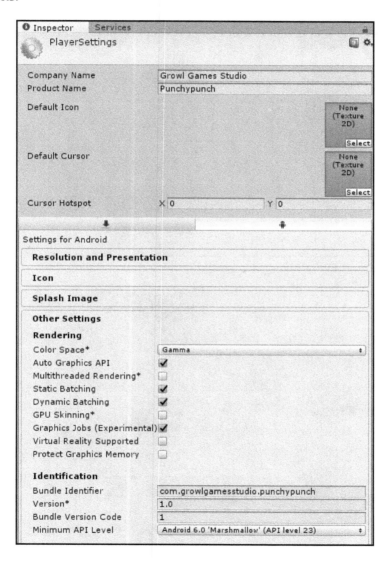

Next under **Publishing Settings** section, we will have to create a new keystore. Type in the password in the **Keystore password** field and confirm the password. Now click on the **Browse Keystore** button and select where you want to store the Keystore. Keep it in a safe place as you might need this file later.

Next under the **Key** section, instead of **Unsigned (debug)** option, click on it and select the **Create a new key** option:

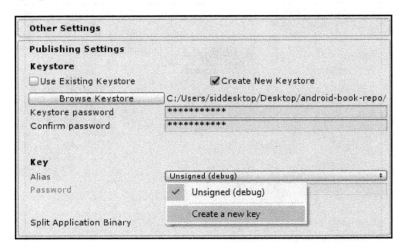

Next fill in the required details:

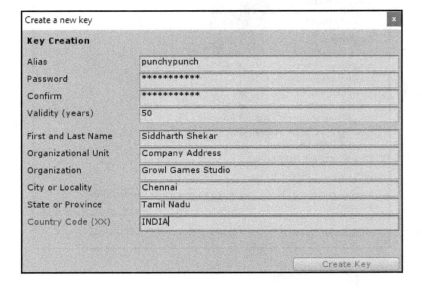

Create an alias, which is usually the name of the product. Create a password for the key and then confirm it. Add in your first name, last name, company address and company name, city, state, and country location.

Now select the alias and type in the password for the key:

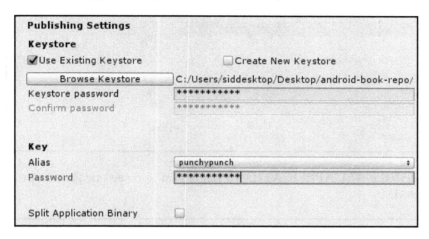

Now we can create an APK to upload. Go to **Build Settings** and click **Build**. It will ask for a location to save the APK, specify a location and name. Remember the location and name:

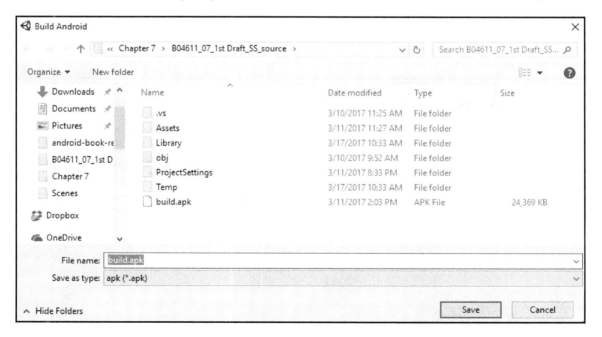

Now go back to the Developer Console. Drag and drop the `build.apk` file onto where it says **Drop your APK file here, or select file**. Once you select the file to upload it will begin:

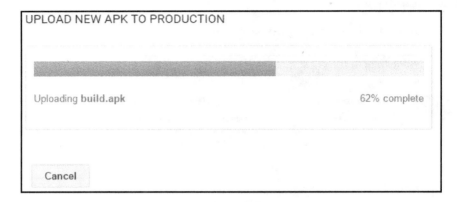

Now, if you go to the **ALL APPLICATIONS** page, you will see our Punchypunch application listed:

Now let us add some achievements.

Adding achievements in the game

In the Developer Console, click on the **GAME SERVICES** tab:

Here click on **+ Add new game** on the top right. Type in the game name and the genre and click on the **Continue** button at the bottom of the screen:

Click on the **ACHIEVEMENTS** tab, and then click **Add achievement** tab. You need to add at least five achievements for it to work.

Type in a name and add a small description. For our example, I am going to add achievements for the number of times the user has played the game. So for playing the game the 1st time, 5th time, 50th, 100th, and 1000th time, I want an achievement to pop up each time:

Next, add a new achievement and all the achievements in:

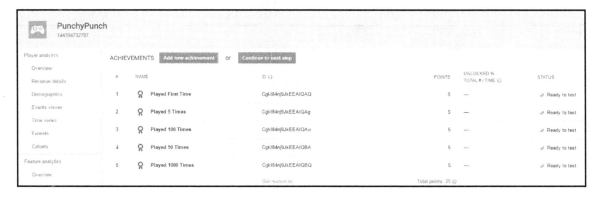

Click on the **Get Resources** button on the bottom and select the **Android** tab in the window. Now, copy all the data:

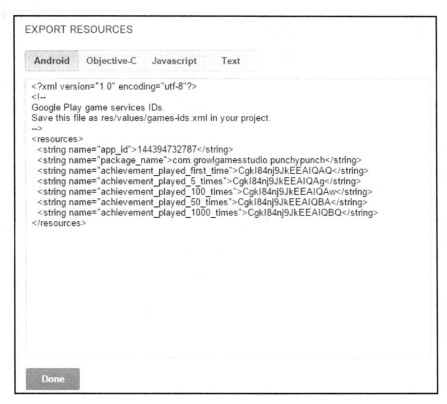

Next go to the **Testing** tab and click on the **Add testers** button. Here add in the e-mail address that you will be using to log in to your device:

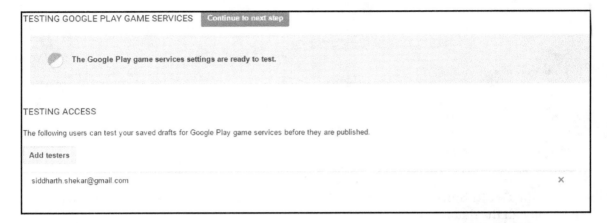

Now you are ready to test the achievements on the device. Go to Unity and go to **Window** | **Google Play Services** | **Setup** | **Android Setup...**:

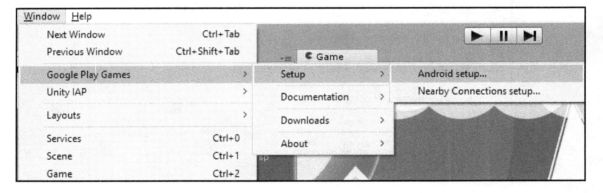

In the window, let the **Directory to save constants** field be set to `Assets` folder.

Type in the details in **Constants class name** component and finally paste the code you copied from **Get Resources** tab here, and click on the **Setup** button at the bottom of the screen:

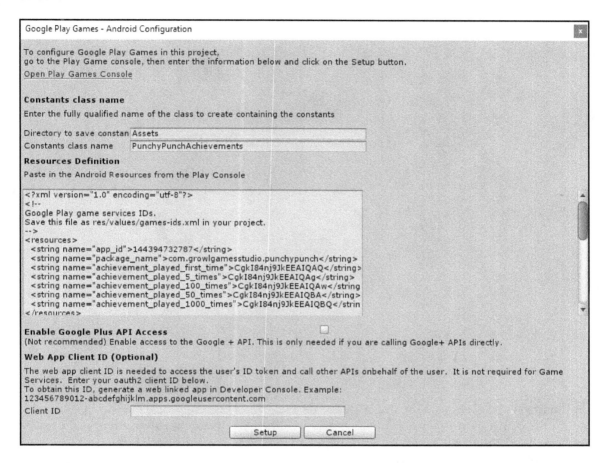

Now when the MainMenu loads, we have to activate Google Play Services and whenever an achievement is hit, we have to send a notification telling Google Play Services that the achievement has been met.

So in the **Project** menu open the MainMenu scene. In the `Project/Scripts` folder create a new script called `MainMenuScript`. In the script, add the following code:

```
using System.Collections;
using System.Collections.Generic;
using UnityEngine;
```

```
using GooglePlayGames;
using UnityEngine.SocialPlatforms;
using GooglePlayGames.BasicApi;

using UnityEngine.UI;

public class mainMenuScript : MonoBehaviour
{
    bool isUserAuthenticated = false;

    // Use this for initialization
    void Start(){
        PlayGamesPlatform.Activate();
        PlayGamesPlatform.DebugLogEnabled = true;
    }

    // Update is called once per frame
    void Update()
    {
        if (!isUserAuthenticated){
            Social.localUser.Authenticate((bool success) => {
                if (success){
                    Debug.Log("You've successfully logged in");
                    isUserAuthenticated = true;
                } else {
                    Debug.Log("Login failed for some reason");
                }
            });
        }
    }
}
```

At the top of the class, add the GooglePlayGames, UnityEngine.SocialPlatform, and System.Collections.Generic namespaces. In the class, create a isUserAthenticated Boolean and initialize it to false. In the Update function, we will check if the user is logged into Google Play Services; otherwise, we will wait until the user is logged in.

We activate the Google Play Services and then enable **Debug** mode. In the Update function, we check if the user is logged in. If the user is logged in, we change our Boolean variable to true, or else we log out saying that the user didn't log in. Attach this script as a component to the MainCamera component in the scene.

Now plug in your device to the computer and go to **Build Settings** and press **Build and Run**. It will connect to the Google Play Services, as shown in the following screenshot:

It will ask you to log in with your e-mail address:

Once you are logged in, it will give you a welcome message:

Now to store information in the achievement that is actually achieved at the gameover condition, add the following:

```
if (playerHealth <= 0 || enemyHealth <= 0) {
    bGameover = true;

    gameOverText.enabled = true;
    resetButton.gameObject.SetActive(true);
    mainMenuButton.gameObject.SetActive(true);

    Instantiate(particlePrefab);
    gameplayCount++;

    if (gameplayCount == 1){
        Social.ReportProgress (PunchyPunchAchievements.
achievement_played_first_time, 100, (bool sucsess) => { });
    } else if (gameplayCount == 5) {
        Social.ReportProgress (PunchyPunchAchievements.
achievement_played_5_times, 100, (bool sucsess) => { });
    } else if (gameplayCount == 50) {
        Social.ReportProgress (PunchyPunchAchievements.
achievement_played_50_times, 100, (bool sucsess) => { });
    } else if (gameplayCount == 100) {
        Social.ReportProgress (PunchyPunchAchievements.
achievement_played_100_times, 100, (bool sucsess) => { });
    } else if (gameplayCount == 1000) {
        Social.ReportProgress (PunchyPunchAchievements.
achievement_played_1000_times, 100,(bool sucsess) => { });
    } else {
        ...
    }
    Debug.Log(" +++++ GAMEOVER ++++");
}
```

In the class add a global integer called `gameplayCount`. When the game is over this variable is incremented.

Depending on the value of the `gameplayCount` variable, the `if` statements are made and the `Social.ProgressReport` function is called. It takes three parameters. The first being is name of the achievement that is stored in the class that was created, the second is the progress level, in this case we will call this when 100% progress is made on the achievement, and the third is a call back function.

Now build and run the game again. Now when you finish the game, you will get the notification that you played for the first time.

Next, we will open the achievements window to see all the achievements. In the MainMenu scene, we have a button that we created to show the achievement.

In the `buttonClick` class, create a new function called `openAchievements`. It is created as follows:

```
public void openAchievements() {
    Social.localUser.Authenticate((bool success) => {
        if (success){
            Debug.Log("You've successfully logged in");
            Social.ShowAchievementsUI();
        } else {
            Debug.Log("Login failed for some reason");
        }
    });
}
```

The `Social.showAchievementsUI()` function opens the **Achievements** window. Now on the **Achievement** button call this function when the button is clicked:

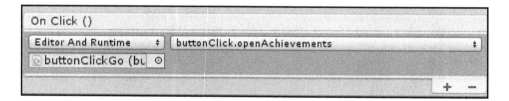

Build and run your project again and click the **Achievement** button on the main menu and the **Achievements** window will pop up, as shown in the following:

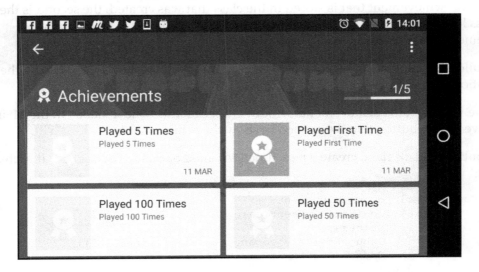

But there is a bit of a problem here. The game only remembers all the information when you play the game; once you close the game, it forgets the information. Let's now see how to store game information on the device.

Saving game stats

Saving game information is actually very easy. This method works on all devices. The `PlayerPrefs` function can save and load player information on the system. All you have to pass in is a key that you will save and retrieve the data and a value that you want to store.

So in your `gameScript`, when you increment the value of `gameplayCount` variable and add the following code after it:

```
PlayerPrefs.SetInt("GameplayCount", gameplayCount);
```

Now the value of `gameplayCount` will be stored in the `GameplayCount` key.

To retrieve information, you will use the `GetInt` function of `PlayerPrefs` to get the value stored in the key. So, before you increment the `gameplayCount` variable, add the following code:

```
int gameplayCount = PlayerPrefs.GetInt("GameplayCount");
```

Now the value stored in the key in the system for `GameplayCount` is retrieved and stored in a local variable called `gameplayCount`.

You are now incrementing this value and then saving the new value in the system. Now the system will remember the number of times you have played the game.

For convenience, I have created a button in the **Options** menu, using which I reset the value of the `GameplayCount` key to `0` whenever the button is pressed:

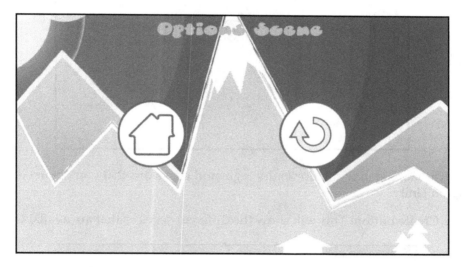

I also added a home button so that I can go back to the main menu. Let us now see how to add ad integration.

Ad integration

In Unity, it is very easy to integrate ads in your games using Unity Ads. In Unity, go to **Windows** | **Services** and a new tab will open on the right:

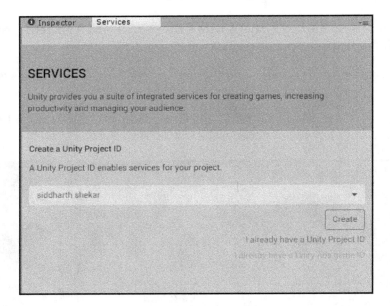

In the **Services** tab, log in with your Unity login and password that you obtained while registering on Unity.

Click on the **Create** button. This will show the different services that are available to you:

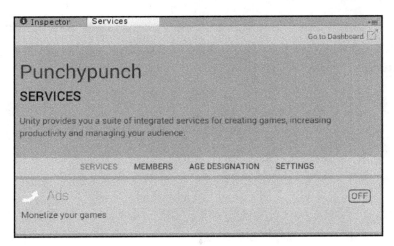

Click on the **SERVICES** tab:

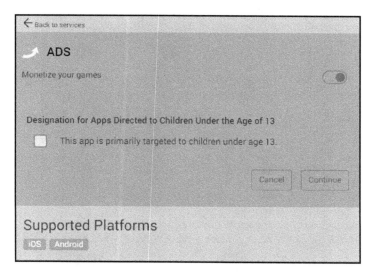

Flip the switch on the top right corner to enable it. If the game is targeted at kids under 13 click the checkbox and click on the **Continue** button:

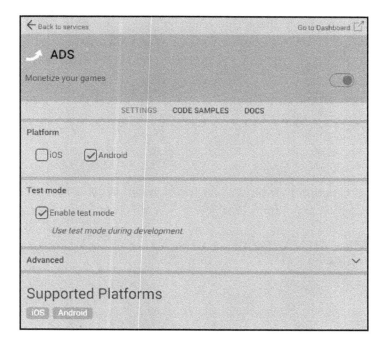

Select **Android** as the target platform, and check the **Enable test mode** option, so that we can test it before we publish the game. Now, in the `gamescript` class, at the top of the class add the following:

```
using UnityEngine.Advertisements;
```

All we have to do is call the `ShowAd` function when we want to show an ad. We don't want to show an ad when the player has an achievement as we also don't want to show the ad every time we call the `ShowAd` function in the `else` statement, when achievements are showing:

```
if (gameplayCount == 1) {
    Social.ReportProgress (PunchyPunchAchievements.
    achievement_played_first_time, 100, (bool sucsess) => { });
}
else if (gameplayCount == 5) {
    Social.ReportProgress (PunchyPunchAchievements.
    achievement_played_5_times, 100, (bool sucsess) => { });
}
else if (gameplayCount == 50) {
    Social.ReportProgress (PunchyPunchAchievements.
    achievement_played_50_times, 100, (bool sucsess) => { });
}
else if (gameplayCount == 100) {
    Social.ReportProgress (PunchyPunchAchievements.
    achievement_played_100_times, 100, (bool sucsess) => { });
}
else if (gameplayCount == 1000) {
    Social.ReportProgress (PunchyPunchAchievements.
    achievement_played_1000_times, 100, (bool sucsess) => { });
} else {
    if (gameplayCount % 3 == 0){
        ShowAd();
    }
}
```

We call the show ad function if `gameplayCount` is divisible by 3. Then, all the magic happens inside the `ShowAd` function.

Create the `ShowAd` function as follows:

```
public void ShowAd()
{
    if (Advertisement.IsReady())
    {
        Advertisement.Show("video", new ShowOptions() {
            resultCallback = adViewResult});
    }
}
```

Sometimes ads are not available at the moment to show, it might be while playing or restarting the game that the ad will start playing. We don't want that so we first check if there is an ad to show so we calling `Advertisement.Isready`.

If there is an ad that is ready, we call the `Advertisement.Show` function, and we specify the type of ad we want to show, which is a video. We add in a callback function that will tell us what the player did while watching an ad or if the ad played at all.

So add a new function called `adViewResult` as follows:

```
public void adViewResult(ShowResult result) {
    switch (result) {
        case ShowResult.Finished:
            Debug.Log(" Player viewed complete Ad"); break;
        case ShowResult.Skipped:
            Debug.Log(" Player Skipped Ad "); break;
        case ShowResult.Failed:
            Debug.Log("Problem showing Ad "); break;
    }
}
```

We check if the ad has finished playing, skipped, or failed. In each case we log out the information. Build and run the game. Now a test ad should show as per our code:

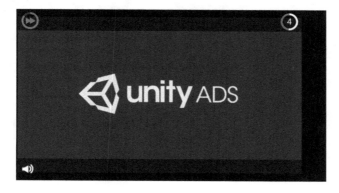

Let us see how to add In-App purchases, so that if the player wants to disable the ad they can make a purchase to disable the ad.

In-App purchasing

In the `Services` tab in Unity, click on `In- App Purchasing` component:

Once again flip the switch on the top right against the **IN-APP PURCHASING** to enable it:

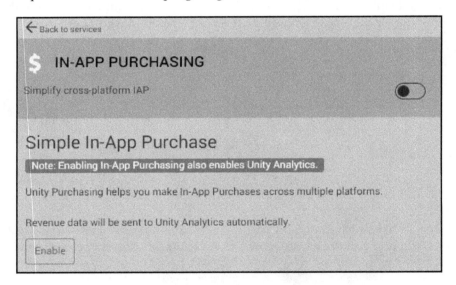

Click on the **Import** button to import the IAP library:

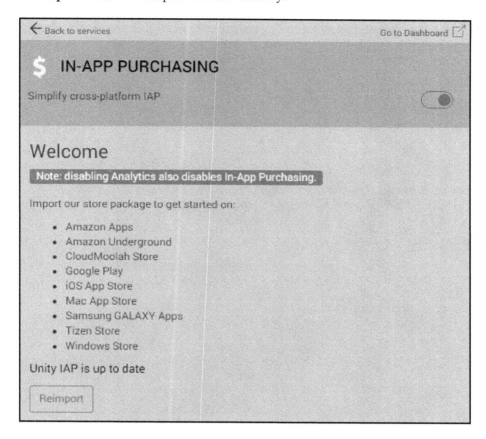

Next, we create a new class that will handle In-App purchases; we will call this class
`IAPManager`.

In this add the following code. The code has been taken from the Unity example site, which has a detailed and commented code showing what each function does. The code can be accessed from `https://unity3d.com/learn/tutorials/topics/ads-analytics/integrating-unity-iap-your-game`:

- InitializePurchasing: Initializes the IAP builder, adds products that are available for sale and supplies a listener to handle purchasing events.
- BuyProductID: A private function which allows us to buy a product we've added using it's product ID string.
- BuyConsumable, BuyNonConsumable, BuySubscription: Public functions which allow us to buy products of different types by passing their respective strings to BuyProductID.
- RestorePurchases: On iOS we can call RestorePurchases to restore products previously purchased.
- OnInitialize: Called to check if the app can connect to Unity IAP or not. OnInitialize will keep trying in the background and will only fail if there is a configuration problem that cannot be recovered from.
- OnInitializeFailed: Called when IAP have failed to initialize and logs a message to the console.
- ProcessPurchase: Checks to see if a product purchase was successful and logs the result to the console.
- OnPurchaseFailed: Logs a message to the console telling us when a purchase failed.

In the Project panel, select the IAPDemo folder, then click the **Create** button and make a new C# script called **Purchaser** and paste-replace the entire contents with the following code:

```C#
using System;
using System.Collections.Generic;
using UnityEngine;
using UnityEngine.Purchasing;

// Placing the Purchaser class in the CompleteProject namespace allows it to interact with ScoreManager,
// one of the existing Survival Shooter scripts.
namespace CompleteProject
{
    // Deriving the Purchaser class from IStoreListener enables it to receive messages from Unity Purchasing.
    public class Purchaser : MonoBehaviour, IStoreListener
    {
        private static IStoreController m_StoreController;        // The Unity Purchasing system.
        private static IExtensionProvider m_StoreExtensionProvider; // The store-specific Purchasing subsystems.
```

The code has been modified for our purpose. As this is a long code, I have added comments with numbers, which I will explain later:

```
using System;
using System.Collections.Generic;
using UnityEngine;
using UnityEngine.Purchasing;

public class IAPManager : MonoBehaviour, IStoreListener
{
    public static IAPManager instance { set; get; }
```

```
        private static IStoreController m_StoreController;
        private static IExtensionProvider m_StoreExtensionProvider;

        public static string kRemoveAds = "removeads"; // 1

        void Awake() {
            instance = this;
        }

        void Start(){
            if (m_StoreController == null){
                InitializePurchasing();
            }
        }

        public void InitializePurchasing(){
            if (IsInitialized()){
                return;
            }
            var builder = ConfigurationBuilder.Instance
(StandardPurchasingModule.Instance());
            builder.AddProduct(kRemoveAds, ProductType.Consumable);// 2
            UnityPurchasing.Initialize(this, builder);
        }

        private bool IsInitialized(){
            return m_StoreController != null && m_StoreExtensionProvider !=
null;
        }

        public void BuyRemoveAds(){
            BuyProductID(kRemoveAds);
        } //3

        void BuyProductID(string productId){
            // If Purchasing has been initialized ...
            if (IsInitialized()){
                Product product = m_StoreController.
                products.WithID(productId);

                if (product != null && product.availableToPurchase){
                    Debug.Log(string.Format("Purchasing product
                    asychronously: '{0}'", product.definition.id));
                    m_StoreController.InitiatePurchase(product);
                }
                else {
                    Debug.Log("BuyProductID: FAIL. Not purchasing product,
either is not found or is not available for purchase");
```

```
            }
        } else {
            Debug.Log("BuyProductID FAIL. Not initialized.");
        }
    }

    public void RestorePurchases()
    {
        // If Purchasing has not yet been set up ...
        if (!IsInitialized()){
            Debug.Log("RestorePurchases FAIL. Not initialized.");
            return;
        }

        if (Application.platform == RuntimePlatform.IPhonePlayer ||
            Application.platform == RuntimePlatform.OSXPlayer) {

            Debug.Log("RestorePurchases started ...");
            var apple = m_StoreExtensionProvider.
GetExtension<IAppleExtensions>();
            apple.RestoreTransactions((result) => {

            Debug.Log("RestorePurchases continuing: " + result + ". If
no further messages, no purchases available to restore.");
            });
        } else {
            Debug.Log("RestorePurchases FAIL. Not supported on this
                    platform. Current = " + Application.platform);
        }
    }

    // --- IStoreListener
    public void OnInitialized (IStoreController controller,
                              IExtensionProvider extensions) {
        Debug.Log("OnInitialized: PASS");
        m_StoreController = controller;
        m_StoreExtensionProvider = extensions;
    }
    public void OnInitializeFailed(InitializationFailureReason error){
        Debug.Log("OnInitializeFailed InitializationFailureReason:" +
                error);
    }

    public PurchaseProcessingResult ProcessPurchase (PurchaseEventArgs
args) {
        if (String.Equals(args.purchasedProduct.definition.id, kRemoveAds,
StringComparison.Ordinal)){
            Debug.Log(string.Format("ProcessPurchase: PASS. Product:
```

```
'{0}'", args.purchasedProduct.definition.id));

            PlayerPrefs.SetInt("noads", 1); //4
            mainMenuScript.noAdsButton.gameObject.SetActive(false);
        } else {
            Debug.Log(string.Format("ProcessPurchase: FAIL. Unrecognized
product: '{0}'", args.purchasedProduct.definition.id));
        }
        return PurchaseProcessingResult.Complete;
    }

    public void OnPurchaseFailed(Product product, PurchaseFailureReason
failureReason) {
        Debug.Log(string.Format("OnPurchaseFailed: FAIL. Product:
                                '{0}', PurchaseFailureReason: {1}",
                                0 product.definition.storeSpecificId,
                                failureReason));
    }
}
```

Products can be of three types: consumable, nonconsumable, and subscription:

- Consumables can be used only once after which you cannot purchase it again
- Nonconsumables can be purchased again and again
- A subscription product is subscription-based like Netflix, which you pay for every month

There are four key steps to remember when setting the product. They are commented in the code as 1, 2, 3, and 4.

First, we set a string that should be the same as what we set in the Android store.

In the initialized `Purchasing` function we have to specify our product as the product needs to be present when the store is built. The store is built every time you click on the store icon.

The Builder will add the product to the store. Specify the product name and type of product here:

```
builder.AddProduct(kRemoveAds, ProductType.Consumable);
```

We will create our own function, which will called when we want to buy a product:

```
public void BuyRemoveAds() {
    BuyProductID(kRemoveAds);
}
```

This intern will call the BuyProductID function in which we pass the product name that will initiate the purchase of the product.

Finally in the initiated function we check if the product was purchased. We set a key so that if the product was purchased the no ads button doesn't show any more:

```
if (String.Equals(args.purchasedProduct.definition.id, kRemoveAds,
                StringComparison.Ordinal)) {
    Debug.Log(string.Format("ProcessPurchase: PASS. Product:
    '{0}'", args.purchasedProduct.definition.id));

    PlayerPrefs.SetInt("noads", 1); //4
    mainMenuScript.noAdsButton.gameObject.SetActive(false);
}
```

Now on the MainMenu scene, create a new button on top-right and in the buttonClick script, add a function that will call the BuyRemoveAds function in the IAPManager class:

```
public void noAdsButton() {
    IAPManager.instance.BuyRemoveAds();
}
```

Also on the mainMenu class add a button object for the Ad remove button and disable it if the noads key is equal to 1.

The mainMenu script should look as follows:

```
using System.Collections;
using System.Collections.Generic;
using UnityEngine;

using GooglePlayGames;
using UnityEngine.SocialPlatforms;
using GooglePlayGames.BasicApi;

using UnityEngine.UI;

public class mainMenuScript : MonoBehaviour
{
    bool isUserAuthenticated = false;
    public static Button noAdsButton;

    // Use this for initialization
    void Start()
    {
        Debug.Log("[Application Launch] Awake");
```

```
PlayGamesPlatform.Activate();
PlayGamesPlatform.DebugLogEnabled = true;

int value = PlayerPrefs.GetInt("noads");
if (value == 1) {
    noAdsButton.gameObject.SetActive(false);
}


}

// Update is called once per frame
void Update()
{
    if (!isUserAuthenticated) {
        Social.localUser.Authenticate((bool success) => {
            if (success){
                Debug.Log("You've successfully logged in");
                isUserAuthenticated = true;
            } else {
                Debug.Log("Login failed for some reason");
            }
        });
    }
}
```

We have to do one final thing. We actually need to add the product in the Developer Console. Go to **All Application | PunchyPunch** and click on **In-app products** option in the list. Now click on **+ Add new product** button:

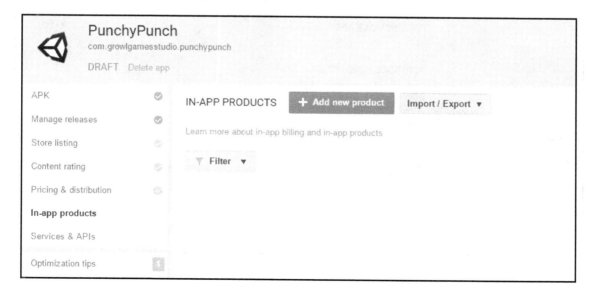

In the box, select **Managed product** option and in the **Product ID** field, add **removeads**. This is the same as the string we set in the `IAPManager` class:

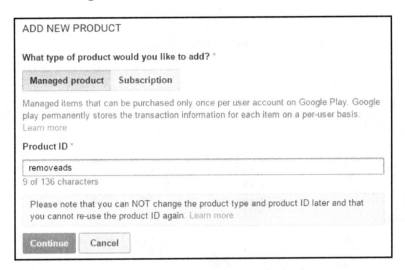

Next, add a title and description in the **Title** and **Description** fields respectively:

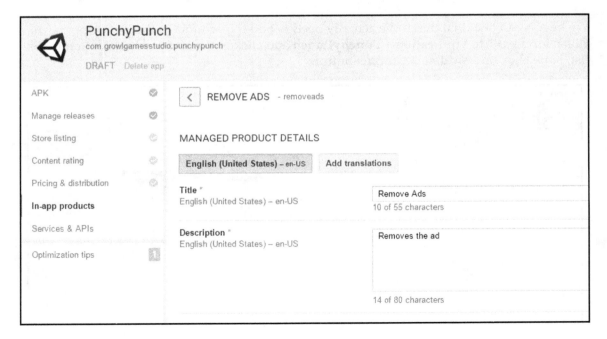

Next, click on **Add a price** button at the bottom and in the **Default price** field, type in the price. In my case it is **INR**, so I will add an appropriate value and click on the **Apply** button:

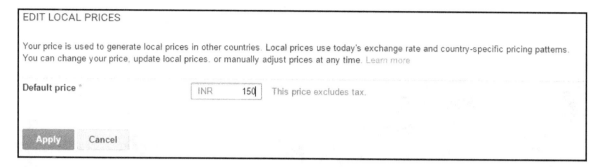

Now the app will show up on the **In-App products**:

You can build and run the app now, but in-app purchases can only be tested once the app has been published. So we will see how it works in the next chapter.

Adding social media integration

First, let us setup a Facebook share integration. Go to `https://developers.facebook.com/` that will open the Facebook developer site. Log in with your Facebook login and password:

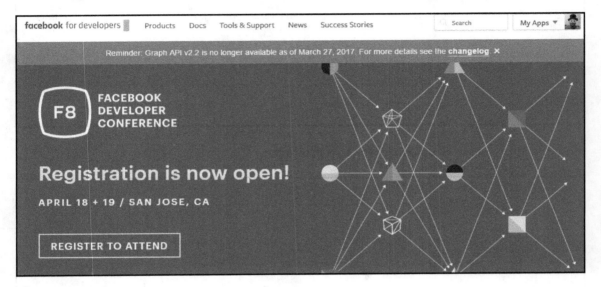

Click on **My Apps** box on the top and select the **Add a New App** option:

Type in the name of the game in the **Display Name** field. Add your contact e-mail address and select **Apps for Pages** option in the **Category** list. Then click on the **Create App ID** button.

In settings click on + **Add Platform** button at the bottom and choose Android. Add the package name for the app and add in the **Class Name** field, which will also be in the reverse website name with the class name at the end. When we create a manager in Unity, we have to make sure that the class name matches this:

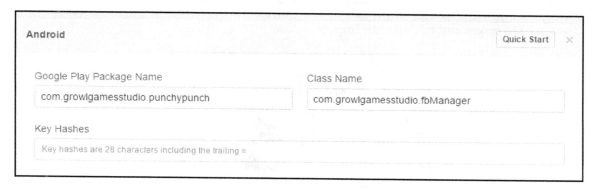

You will also get an App ID, copy this information as this will be required. Next on the top-right corner, there is a button called **DOCs**, click it as we will need to download the Facebook SDK for Unity. Click on Unity SDK from the list and the SDK will start downloading:

Product Docs	SDKs	Platforms
Account Kit	Android SDK	iOS Developers
Analytics for Apps	iOS SDK	Add Facebook to your iOS app.
App Ads	Swift SDK	Android Developers
App Development	React Native SDK	Add Facebook to your Android app.
App Invites	JavaScript SDK	Web Developers
App Links	PHP SDK	Add Facebook to your site or web app.
Atlas API	tvOS SDK	
Facebook Audience Network	Unity SDK	

Once the SDK is downloaded, make sure your current unity project is open and import the package:

Check all the boxes and click on the **Import** button:

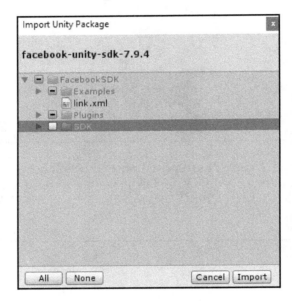

You will see that there is a new **Facebook** tab on your project, click on it and select **Edit Settings** options:

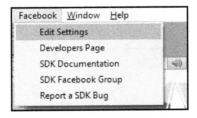

In the **Inspector** type, the **App Name (Optional)** and **App ID [?]** fields are as it appears on the Facebook Developer Console:

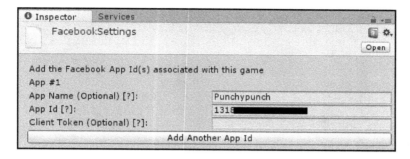

Next, create a new class called `fbManager`. In the class, add the following code:

```
using System.Collections;
using System.Collections.Generic;
using UnityEngine;

using Facebook.Unity;
using System.Linq;

public class fbManager : MonoBehaviour
{
    void Awake() {
        if (!FB.IsInitialized) {
            FB.Init();
        } else {
            FB.ActivateApp();
        }
    }

    public void Share() {
        if (FB.IsLoggedIn)
        {
            FB.ShareLink(contentTitle: "Growl Games Studio",
                contentURL: new System.Uri
                ("http://www.growlgamesstudio.com"),
                contentDescription: "Like and Share my page",
                callback: onShare);
        } else {
            // Debug.Log("User Cancelled Login");
            FB.LogInWithReadPermissions(null, callback: onLogin);
        }
    }
}
```

```
        private void onLogin(ILoginResult result) {
            if (result.Cancelled)
            {
                Debug.Log(" user cancelled login");
            }
            else {
                Share();
            }
        }

        private void onShare(IShareResult result) {
            if (result.Cancelled || !string.IsNullOrEmpty
                (result.Error))
            {
                Debug.Log("sharelink error: " + result.Error);
            } else if(!string.IsNullOrEmpty(result.PostId)) {
                ...
            }
        }
    } // class
```

In the `Awake` function, first we check whether Facebook SDK is initialized. If not then we initialize it and we activate the app.

The `Share` function is the function that we will call when the Facebook button is pressed from the main menu.

Once the button is pressed, the function will check whether the user is logged in. If they are logged in then the post is made using the `sharelink` function. We pass in the content title, a link to the website, and a description. We also provide a call back function that will check if the post was made or not.

If the user is not logged in then, we log in using the `loginWithPermissions` function. We also pass in a call back function that will check if the user has logged in. Once the user is logged in the function will call the share function.

While sharing if it was cancelled the `onShare` call back function will specify if there is an error, otherwise it will post a message. Now create a new button in the MainMenu for Facebook sharing and call the `Share` function once the button is pressed.

You also need to install **openSSL** as it is a requirement for Facebook. Download and install OpenSSL from `https://code.google.com/archive/p/openssl-for-windows/downloads`. Download, unzip, and install it. Next, go to Start and search for `Environment Variables`. Open it.

Under the **System Variables** section, look for the path and press **Edit**.

Under **Edit Environment Variables**, click New and type in the OpenSSL binary location. Click OK. Next click New again and add the JDK binary location. Click **OK** and exit:

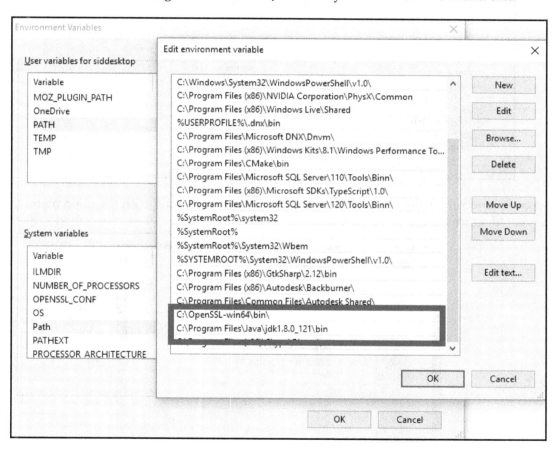

You might get build errors as when you installed Facebook SDK there might be older versions of `support-annotations-23.4.0.jar` and `support-v4-23.4.0.aar` library present. You will have to manually go into the Facebook Android library folder and delete these files. So go to the location and delete the files:

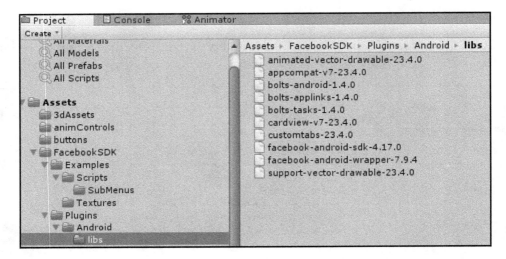

Now build and run the application and click on the Facebook button on the main menu that you created. Once logged in you are ready to post on Facebook:

Next we will look at Twitter sharing. Twitter sharing is really easy. Create one more button on the MainMenu for calling Twitter share and attach a function that will get called once the button is pressed. I created a function called `openTwitter` in the `buttonClick` class as follows:

```
public void openTwitter() {
    string appStoreLink =
    "https://play.google.com/store/apps/details?
    id=com.growlgamesstudio.pizZapMania";

    string twitterAddress = "http://twitter.com/intent/tweet";
    string descriptionParameter = "Punchy Punch";
    string message = "GET THIS AWESOME GAME";//text string

    Application.OpenURL(twitterAddress + "?text=" +
        WWW.EscapeURL(message + "n" + descriptionParameter + "n"
        + appStoreLink));
}
```

You will create strings that will store values for app store links, the twitter tweet intent address link, a description, and a message. Then you will call `Application.OpenURL` and pass the information as a string.

Now, when you build the application and press the Twitter button, you will be able to share a tweet:

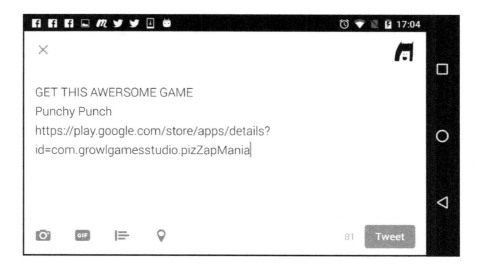

Summary

In this chapter, we added sound and added touch input as we have only worked with mouse clicks all this time.

We also created a developer account and made the app itself ready. We saw how to run the app on a device. We also created the app on the store and uploaded the APK to the store. We added achievements by saving the number of times we played the game. We added IAP and ads so that we can monetize the game. In the next chapter, we will finally publish the game.

8
Sound, Finishing Touches, and Publishing

In this chapter, we will add sound and see how to make the same app run on different Android device resolutions. We will optimize the APK so that the file size is smaller. We will then prepare the app itself for publishing by adding icons. We will also prepare the app store itself by adding icons and screenshots and finally push the publish button so that the app is published.

This chapter includes the following topics:

- Adding sound
- Handling multiple resolution
- Optimizing the APK size
- Preparing for publishing
- Publishing the game

Adding sound

For adding sounds, the files are included in the `Resources` folder for this chapter. There are three files in total, of which two are sounds effects and one is a music file. The sounds effects are to be used in the game.

The punch sound is to be played when whether the enemy or the player gets hit. The block sound is to be played when the player or the enemy blocks the attack. The `bgMusic` file is the background music file that is to be played when any scene loads. Drag the `Audio` folder into the project.

Now open the MainMenu scene. And drag the `bgMusic` file into the scene. Take a look at the **Inspector** pane:

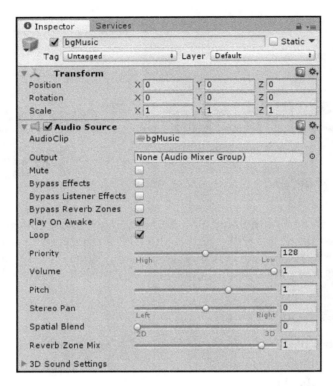

The position of the background music doesn't matter, but if you were using the sound for ambience then make sure that you set the location of the sound source.

The **Play On Awake** option is checked by default, which is what we want. However, we also want the music to be looped, so make sure to check the **Loop** checkbox as well.

If you play the scene, you will hear the sound playing automatically. Do the same for game and options scenes as well. Let's see how to add the punch and block sound effect.

Whenever we click a button, it is good to give an audio feedback to the player so that they know that the button was clicked.

For this, drag and drop the punch audio effect into the scene as well. Make sure that none of the options such as **Play On Awake** are checked on the effect as it would start playing when the scene starts and we don't want that:

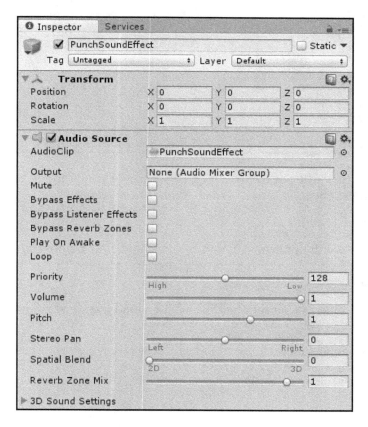

We will be playing the sound via the script. Open the `buttonClicks.cs` file. At the top of the class, create a public variable of type `AudioSource` called `punchSound`, as shown in the following code:

```
public class buttonClick : MonoBehaviour {
    public AudioSource punchSound;
    public IAPManager iapManager;
```

Go to **GameObject** onto which the script is attached and attach the punch effect to the punch audio source:

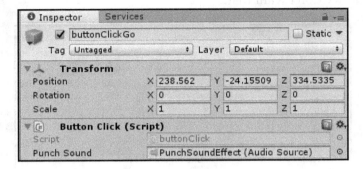

Now, you can call the audio source to be played wherever you want. Suppose, we call the function in the `onButtonClick` class, which loads a new scene:

```
punchSound.Play();
```

But, if you add it you will not hear when the scene changes as before the sound even plays, the game scene loads and you won't hear the punch sound effect. So we will make some changes to the function.

We will use a co-routine to wait for a while and then load the scene so that the sound effect plays:

```
public void onButtonClick (string level){
    punchSound.Play();
    StartCoroutine (onSceneLoad(level));
}

IEnumerator onSceneLoad (string sceneName) {
    yield return new WaitForSeconds(0.5f);
    SceneManager.LoadScene(sceneName);
}
```

So, in the `onButtonClick` function, we start a new co-routine and pass in the function we want to call. Then we create a function to be called, which needs to return an `IEnumerator`.

We then wait for half a second, call the `SceneManager.LoadScene` function, and then pass in the level name string to load the level.

This can be done to the other functions as well while pressing the Achievements, Facebook, and Twitter buttons. I shall leave that up to you guys as you'll gain exercise using it. This also needs to be done for other buttons on other scenes as well.

Now, let's see how to add the sound effect during gameplay. In the startScene, load both the sound effects into the scene and disable play on awake for both files. In the playerScript, add public variables for the punch and block sound effects:

```
float totalTime = 0.0f;
float timeSinceLastHit = 0.0f;
float hitTimeInterval = 30.0f * .016f;

float screenWidth = Screen.width;

public AudioSource punchSound;
public AudioSource blockSound;
```

On **theDude** game object on which the playerScript is attached link the punch and block sounds:

Now, whenever the player gets hit we have to play the punch sound effect and if the player is blocking we play the block sound effect. So, open the playerScript and where we check if the enemy is punching we make the following changes to the code:

```
if (eScript.isPunching == true) {
    if (anim.GetBool("bIsDefending") == false) {
        //Debug.Log("player got hit");
        anim.SetTrigger("tGotHit");
        health -= eScript.damage;
        Debug.Log("Player Health: " + health);
```

```
        punchSound.Play();
    } else {
        blockSound.Play();
    }
}
```

effects playing as it should. Let's do the same for the enemy as well, as follows:

When you play the game you will find the sound effects playing as it should. Let's do the same for the enemy as well, as follows:

```
if (pAnim.GetBool("tIsPunching")) {
    if (anim.GetBool("bEnemyIsDefending") == false) {
    // Debug.Log("enemy got hit");
    anim.SetTrigger("tEnemyGotHit");
    anim.SetBool("bEnemyIsDefending", true);
    health -= pScript.damage;
    Debug.Log("Enemy Health: " + health);
    punchSound.Play();
    } else {
        blockSound.Play();
    }
}
```

Handling multiple resolutions

Handling multiple resolutions is very easy in Unity. Open the MainMenu Scene. In the Hierarchy select the **Canvas** component:

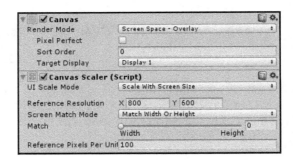

The **Canvas Scaler** component is responsible for scaling the UI canvas depending upon the width and height of the screen. Set the **UI Scale Mode** field to **Scale With Screen Size**. This will scale the UI elements depending upon the width and height of the screen.

We also give a reference resolution based on which the UI will be scaled. Here it is 800x600. If it can fit the UI in that resolution, then it will definitely be able to fit in the 16:9 resolutions as well.

The next parameter is the **Match** parameter. Here we set the width to match and then the height will be scaled accordingly. This would have to be declined for all the canvas in the other scenes. Once you do this the game should be able to scale the UI depending upon the screen resolution.

Optimizing the APK

To get the individual file size, we make use of the console in Unity. Click on the small down arrow on the top-right of the console and select **Open Editor Log**:

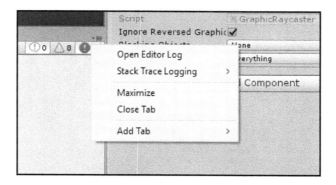

This will open a text file with the log information. Scroll down in the text file to where it shows the size of the individual files. As you can see, Unity already does a good job of removing assets that are not being used in the current game.

It also breaks down the assets and shows which of the assets are contributing to the size. Here we see that the `menuImage.jpg`, `ground.jpg`, and `wall.jpg` images are quite big in size:

```
Editor.log - Notepad                                                    —    □    ×
File  Edit  Format  View  Help

Unloading 117 unused Assets to reduce memory usage. Loaded Objects now: 3074.
Total: 20.783979 ms (FindLiveObjects: 0.214747 ms CreateObjectMapping: 0.029842 ms MarkObjects: 7.414929 ms  DeleteObjects:

WARNING: Shader Unsupported: 'VR/SpatialMapping/Wireframe' - Pass '' has no vertex shader
WARNING: Shader Unsupported: 'VR/SpatialMapping/Wireframe' - Setting to default shader.
Compressed shader 'Standard' on gles from 0.75MB to 0.06MB
Compressed shader 'Standard' on gles3 from 1.26MB to 0.08MB

Textures       6.8 mb     52.1%
Meshes         62.2 kb    0.5%
Animations     45.5 kb    0.3%
Sounds         397.3 kb   3.0%
Shaders        233.0 kb   1.8%
Other Assets   97.5 kb    0.7%
Levels         175.5 kb   1.3%
Scripts        1.3 mb     9.6%
Included DLLs  3.9 mb     30.3%
File headers   38.0 kb    0.3%
Complete size  13.0 mb    100.0%

Used Assets and files from the Resources folder, sorted by uncompressed size:
2.6 mb   20.3% Assets/images/menuImage.jpg
1.5 mb   11.3% Assets/images/ground.jpg
1.5 mb   11.3% Assets/images/wall.jpg
382.5 kb        2.9% Assets/Audio/bgMusic.mp3
294.3 kb        2.2% Resources/unity_builtin_extra
252.6 kb        1.9% Assets/buttons/homeBtn2.png
252.6 kb        1.9% Assets/buttons/resetBtn2.png
252.6 kb        1.9% Assets/buttons/pauseBtnOFF.png
111.2 kb        0.8% Assets/3dAssets/theDude.FBX
88.6 kb         0.7% Assets/buttons/noads.png
69.5 kb         0.5% Assets/buttons/achBtn.png
64.6 kb         0.5% Assets/buttons/twitter.png
58.7 kb         0.4% Assets/buttons/playBtn_pressed-ipad.png
58.7 kb         0.4% Assets/buttons/playBtn_normal-ipad.png
39.4 kb         0.3% Assets/buttons/facebook.png
29.0 kb         0.2% Assets/fonts/duncecapbb_reg.ttf
```

One of the popular tools for reducing the size of a JPEG is **Paint.NET**; it is a free application to reduce the file size. You can download the tool from `http://www.getpaint.net/index.html`.

Similarly, for of PNG images, you can use the **PNG Crush** tool to reduce the size of the image. It can be downloaded from `https://pmt.sourceforge.io/pngcrush`.

On the whole, it is recommended to use vector art as much as possible instead of raster images as the image quality will be crisp irrespective of the resolution and it will also save space for optimization purposes.

Preparing the build for publishing

One thing that we still haven't done is to add the icon for the app. Once you have the app icon designed we set the icon for different Android devices.

For creating different size app icons from a single image, I use the `http://makeappicon.com/` website. All you have to do is drop the icon design in there and it will generate the icons of different sizes. Either browse to the file on the icon folder or drag and drop onto the link on the site and it will generate the icon and then it can be e-mailed to you:

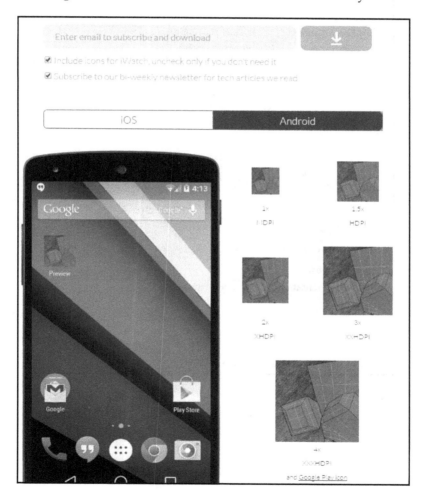

Once you receive the files, download and extract them in a new folder called `Icons` in the `Project` folder.

Open **PlayerSettings** in Unity. Under PlayerSettings, you can add the company logo. Make sure you add the details in the **Company Name** and **Product Name** fields. Under **Resolution and Presentation** section, set **Default Orientation*** field to **Landscape Left**:

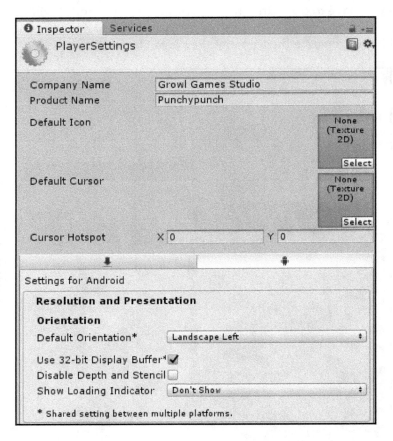

Next, under the **Icon** component, check the **Override for Android** option and select the icon with the correct resolution:

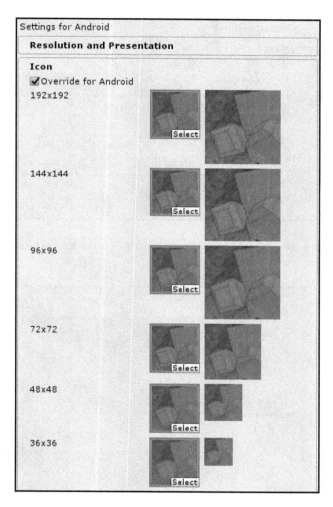

Next is the splash screen section. If you are a Unity pro user, then you will be able to select the splash screen of your choice. Otherwise, you can leave it empty. Next, in **Other Settings** field make sure you have added the correct package name, version, and bundle version code.

For minimum API level, I have selected 4.0 as I want to target as many users as possible, but make sure the game works well on an actual device before setting the minimum API level. Keep the rest of the settings as they are.

Next in **Publishing Settings**, select your **Keystore** and type in the password. Select the alias for the key and type the password for it in the **Keystore password**:

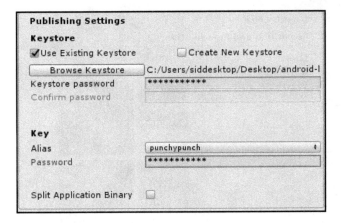

Next, open Services and select the ADS link and uncheck the**Enable test mode** option to disable the testing:

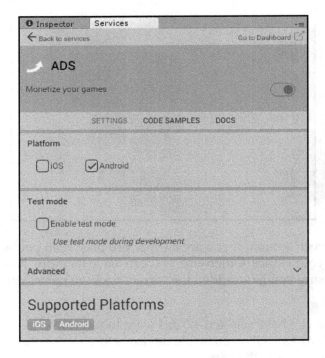

Now open **Build Settings** and build the APK to upload to the store.

Publishing the game

Open the Android Developer Console, select **All Applications**, and select the app that you would like to publish. Upload the new APK to the site.

Next, we have to make sure that all the sections are checked with a green tick mark as we publish the game only after this is done:

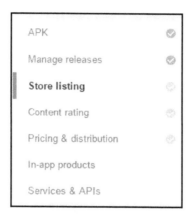

So select the **Store listing** link and fill in the **Title**, **Short Description**, and **Full Description** fields:

- The **Title** field takes the name of the game that will be displayed on the app store, so make sure the name is unique, catchy, and easy to remember.
- The **Short Description** is shown on the store as well. The short description is more like a sneak peak into what the game/asp is about. Usually, you will specify the USP of the product telling the reader what makes your game appealing and different from other products. You will also specify the genre of the game here so that if the reader is into that genre then they can read further about it. Once the user clicks the link it will reveal the full description.

- In the **Full Description** field, you should tell what the game has to offer to the reader. This includes features and a short summary of the story and player motivation, and so on. I have provided a short example in the following screenshot:

Scrolling further down we have to provide icons, screenshots, and feature graphics. I really can't emphasize how important the icons and selection of screenshots are to the success of your game.

Icons need to be on top of our priority list as it is the first thing the user will see once they come across the app. It becomes even more important given the fact that there are tons of apps getting released on the app store on a daily basis. A lot of thought and effort needs to be put into selecting the right kind of icon that can summarize the gist of your game and at the same time is unique enough to differentiate itself from the millions of icons on the app store.

Once the user is interested in the icon and clicks on it, the next thing that will grab their attention is the screenshots. A minimum of three screenshots need to be uploaded. You can upload more than that. Pick and select the images for your screenshot that complement what you say in the full description. For each bullet point in the feature, provide a screenshot to tell the user what you are offering.

If you are targeting tablets, add screenshots specially taken on tablets. Also, if you are developing for Android TV and Google Daydream, add screenshots for that as well.

You can also link a promo video that you have on YouTube. Make sure the video is not more than 30 seconds:

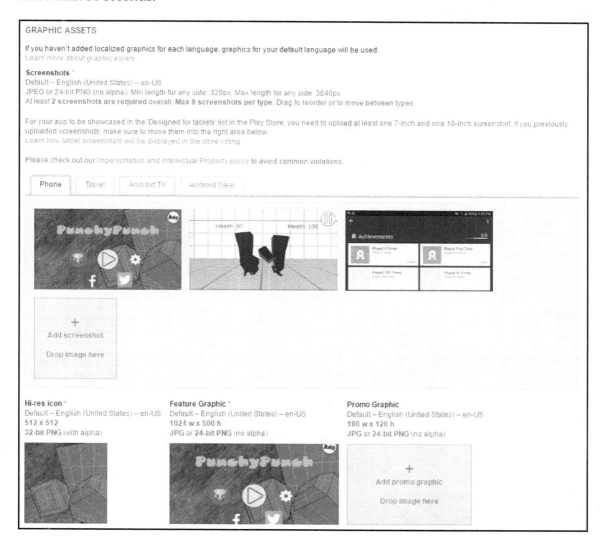

Next fill out the details in the **Categorization** section. Here you will specify if it is an application or a game and what genre. Provide your company website, e-mail address, and submit a privacy policy.

If you are not submitting a privacy policy, you can uncheck the box under the **Privacy Policy** section to say that you are not:

Once all the information is filled correctly to your satisfaction, click the **Save Draft** button on the top-right corner of the page. Next, let's move on to the content rating section.

Here you will make sure that the content doesn't include offensive material and the quality of the product is up to the **International Age Rating Coalition (IARC)** rating standards. IARC is a body that assigns ratings to a given app or mobile games. Click on the Continue button to proceed.

Fill out your e-mail address, so that if an issue is encountered in the game, IARC can get in touch with you for clarification. Next, select the app category and, in that, select **Game**.

Under the **Game** category, you have to mention that your game doesn't include material pertaining to violence, fear, sexuality, gambling, language, controlled substances, crude humor, and other miscellaneous things. Specify **No** option for all the items up until Crude Humor, as shown in the following screenshot:

For the **MISCELLANEOUS** category, we specify **No** to all items except digital purchase:

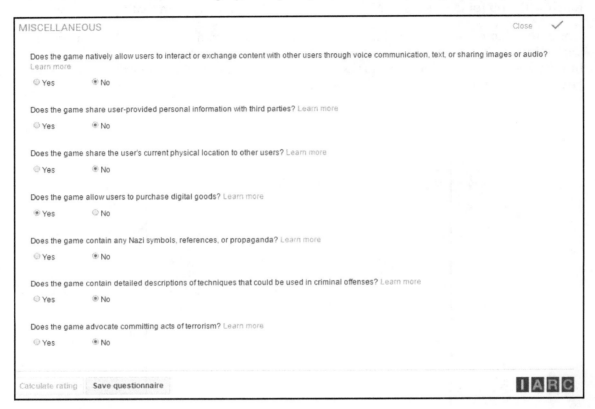

Since we have in-app purchases, we have to specify **Yes** for that. Once done, save it by clicking on the **Save Questionnaire** option. Next, click **Calculate rating** tab, following screen will be displayed:

CONTENT RATING

GAME
App is a game.

QUESTIONNAIRE SUMMARY

MISCELLANEOUS

• Can purchase digital goods

CALCULATED RATING Learn more

Rating System	Rating Category	Descriptors
Australian Classification Board (ACB) Australia	General	General
Classificação Indicativa (ClassInd) Brazil	All ages	
Entertainment Software Rating Board (ESRB) North America	Everyone	
Pan-European Game Information (PEGI) Europe	PEGI 3	
Unterhaltungssoftware Selbstkontrolle (USK) Germany	USK: All ages	
IARC Generic Rest of world	Rated for 3+	
Google Play South Korea	Rated for 3+	

A game unsuitable for minors younger than 18 may be removed from Google Play in Korea unless pre-rated by GRAC. Please see here for more detail.

You will then get a summary and a rating for the game. The same will also be e-mailed to you at the address provided.

Next, click on **Apply Rating**; you will see that your rating is set. Click on **PRICING & DISTRIBUTION** and you will see the following window:

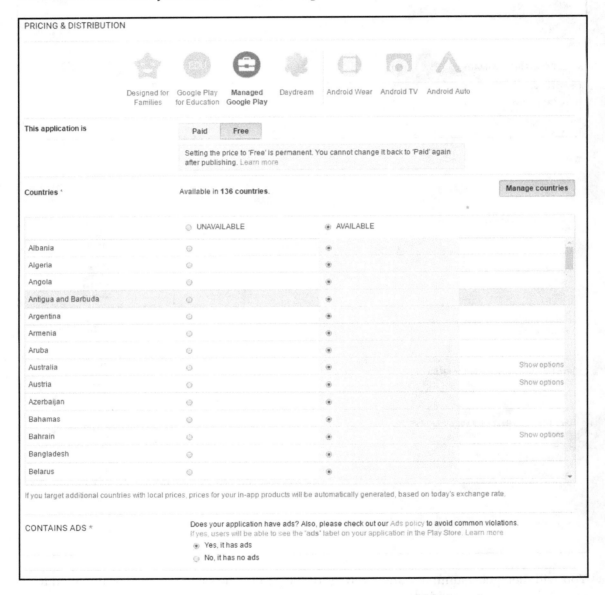

Here, select if you want the app to be free or paid. If you choose for it to be paid, then specify the price that you want to sell the app at.

Click on all the countries that you want the game to sell in. Clicking the **Available** option will select all countries from the list. You can deselect the countries that you don't want the app to be distributed in. Also, at the bottom select that the app contains ads in the **CONTAINS ADS** field.

Check the **CONSENT** check list, shown in the following screenshot, if you approve the app to be promoted outside the Google Play Store, and that the app complies with Android Content Guidelines and US Export laws:

Click the **Save Draft** button on the top-right corner of the screen. We already have specified in-app products, services and APIs, so we don't have to do anything here. But we have to go to Game Services and publish the achievements. So go to **Game Services** and select the app.

Provide the detail in **Display Name** and **Description** fields on the main page and upload the icon and feature graphics here as well:

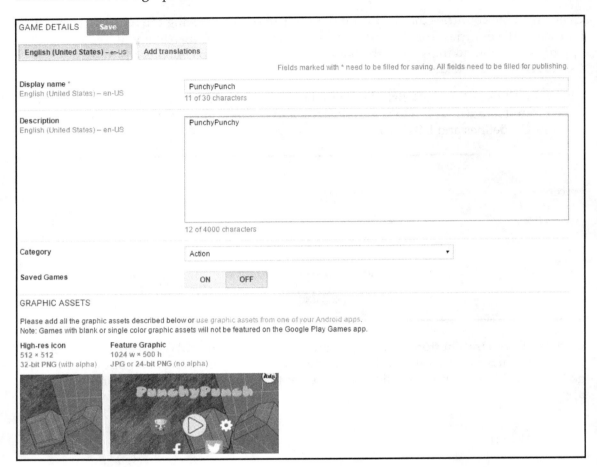

Click the **Save** button on the top-left corner of the window. Next, go to the
ACHIEVEMENTS tab, select each achievement, and add the icons:

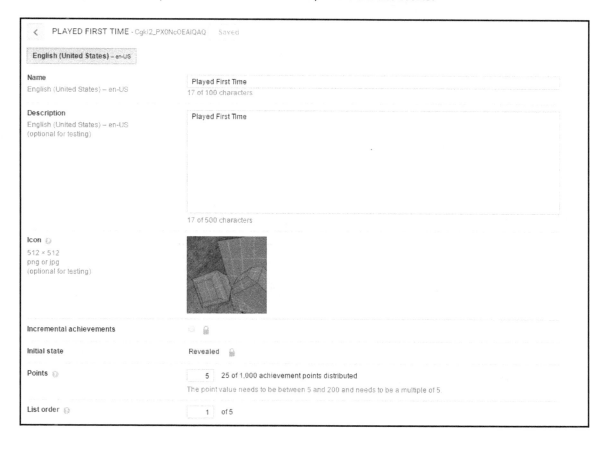

Once you have added icons for all the achievements, you will have the option to publish the game at the top-right corner. Once published, your achievement page will look like the following:

Now we can publish the app itself. Go to **All Applications** and select **Manage releases**. It will show that you have an app that is ready for production:

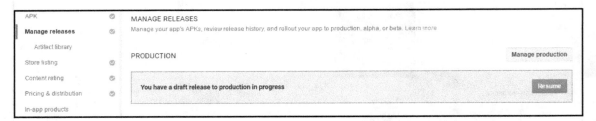

Click on the **Resume** button. Add the detail in the **RELEASE NAME** section and add a description to show what's new in this release:

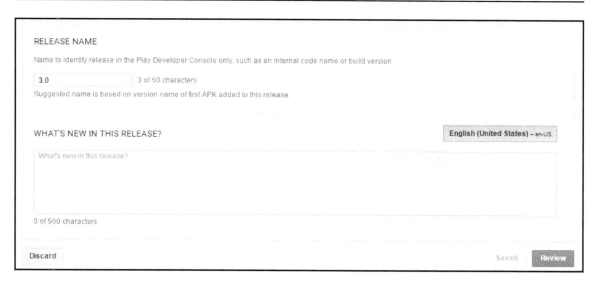

Click on the **Review** button and then click on**Start Rollout to Production**. You will be asked to confirm that the app will now be available on the app store:

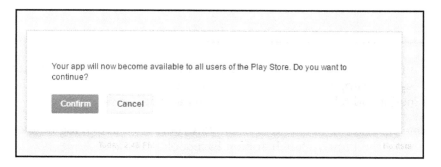

Click on the **Confirm** button and now it will show you that the app is now pending for publication:

It takes about an hour for the app to be published and about three to four hours to be properly visible on the app store. So, be patient. Once it is released, you can distribute the link on social media and tell your friends to download and rate it.

There is still one small thing to take care of on Facebook. We have to log in to our developer account and enable the PunchyPunch app on Facebook.

Go to the Facebook developer account and select the app. Now go to **App Review** tab and under the option saying **Make Punchypunch Public**, flip the switch to make it public.

Now the app is public and your friends can share your game:

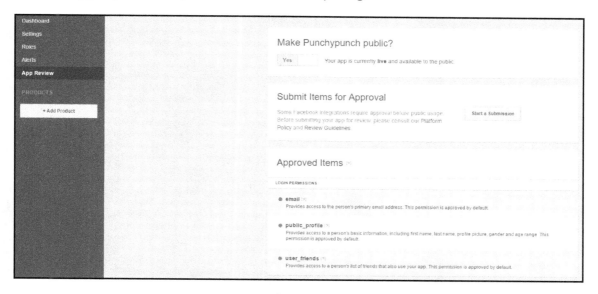

Congratulations! You have successfully developed an Android app on Unity and published it on the Google Play Store.

Summary

In this chapter, we added sound to the game, prepared the app for publishing, and made changes to the app store itself. We uploaded the final build and published the app itself on to the store.

Index

9 781783 550777